**DATE DUE**

| | | | |
|---|---|---|---|
| AUG 22 2002 | | | |
| OCT 04 2002 | | | |
| MAR 10 2018 | | | |
| | | | |
| | | | |
| | | | |
| | | | |
| | | | |
| | | | |
| | | | |
| | | | |
| | | | |
| | | | |
| | | | |

W9-DGV-135

#47-0108 Peel Off Pressure Sensitive

# Late
# Bloomers

# Coming of Age
## in Today's America:
## The Right Place at the Wrong Time

TIMES BOOKS

RANDOM HOUSE

# Late Bloomers

David Lipsky and Alexander Abrams

Owing to limitations of space, permission acknowledgments appear
on page 225.

Library of Congress Cataloging-in-Publication Data
Lipsky, David. 1965–.
Late bloomers: coming of age in today's America: the right place at the wrong
time / by David Lipsky and Alexander Abrams.
p.   cm.
ISBN 0-8129-2290-5
1. Young adults—United States—Psychology. 2. Adult children—United States.
3. College graduates—United States. 4. United States—Social conditions—
1980– . I. Abrams, Alexander. II. Title.
HQ799.7.L57 1994
305.24'2'0973—dc20   94-15951

Manufactured in the United States of America
9 8 7 6 5 4 3 2
First Edition

Book design by Claire Naylon Vaccaro

I am experiencing a need which everyone of our age
feels to some extent with relation to society. I feel
the need of "becoming established."

—*Gustave Flaubert, at twenty-eight*

# acknowledgments

First and foremost, our editor, Peter Smith, for his dedication and energy and good sense throughout the project, and for his many close and intelligent readings. This book could not have been written without him. I would also like to thank our agent, Suzanne Gluck, for her good ideas and her great savvy and input; Susan Jensen, for her wonderful attention to all the details we otherwise would have missed; Deb Futter, for her gift of patience (and time, especially of time); Peter Osnos, for seeing the book from beginning to completion; Sloan Harris, for valuable impressions on the generation; Beth Pearson, for helping us meet a tight deadline; and Mary Beth Roche and Jessica Reighard, for their energy and good ideas and support. They are the best friends a book could have.

Thanks also to the many friends who read this book at its various stages and offered their various kinds of aid: Evelyn Shapiro, David Samuels, Faith Kelleher, Stephen Ramsey, Pat Sutton, Tristan Davies, Jonathan Lipsky, and Elizabeth Wurtzel. I would also like to thank the many friends and strangers who bravely shared their impressions with us—at great expense of time, with no reward but gratitude—and whose experiences went very far toward making up the bulk of this book.

—David Lipsky

# acknowledgments

I would like to thank my parents, Robert and Natalie, and my brother and sister, Peter and Jacqueline, without whose love and support this book would not have been possible. I would also like to thank Marcella Goheen, who has been a true friend throughout this period. And I would like to acknowledge the many friends and acquaintances, personal and professional, whose contributions have made *Late Bloomers* a reality. They include Peter Smith, Peter Osnos, Jessica Reighard, and Mary Beth Roche at Times Books; Suzanne Gluck, Susan Jensen, Trica Davey, Sloan Harris, Herb Cheyette, Brian Alexander, Heather Schroeder, Elizabeth Bennett, and Jill Jones at ICM; Mara Manus, Jonathan Taplin, and Lisa Grundy at Trans Pacific Films; Don Epstein and David Kushner at Greater Talent Network; Brian Segall and Scott Rosenblum of Kramer, Levin; Jed Alpert of Warren, Alpert, Beigelman & Indig; Michael Collins of Third Millenium; Jason Weinberg; David Klinghoffer; D. J. Paul; Eric Avram; Peter Bloch; Jennifer Karady; Michele Rosenthal; Arthur Liman; Davis Guggenheim; Phil Sutfin; Mara Berkman; Ken Gellman; Charles Feldman; David Shipley; and Sonja Weinkopf.

—Alexander Abrams

# contents

# Late
# Bloomers

# a meditation

Think of the twentysomethings you know. Aren't they just the tiniest bit . . . *disappointing?*

If you're a parent, and you're speaking to your children by phone, aren't there moments—when they're talking about their jobs, or their apartments—when the conversation seems to hang, when you feel them grasping for the best way to present their lives to you? When their voices turn *unnatural,* so you sense they are asking you with their voices not to talk about these topics? Or, the reverse—no matter how carefully you hew to "successful" or "safe" topics (the achievements of an older sibling, or of a younger one still in school), you hear a different kind of catch in your kid's voice? That's when you know. They're going to ask for money. No matter where you try to steer the conversation next—your own hazards at work, a movie they really ought to see, politics when all else fails—the voice on the other end pauses, doesn't seem to be listening. "Sure, sure," they say. And then they ask—because the phone is going to be shut off if they can't put something together, or they need a new suit for an interview. You say yes—whether money is an easy subject for you or not—and then all at once the sun comes out again. You've given him money, and you've brought him back. Maybe she's twenty-five, or twenty-nine, or twenty-one. And when he hangs up, you're the one left with a little burden, a little catch of *something* in your chest. She isn't quite making it through the world the way you think she ought to. She's fiscally sloppy in some way. For some reason he doesn't yet know the ropes. Your kid is the age you were when he was five or six, and sounds so much younger than you did then.

Or maybe you're a twentysomething yourself—and the word itself makes you cringe. You wince before using it, and you wince when you hear it about to come plopping out of someone else's mouth. Look at your friends—or your own apartment, or your own phone bill. Aren't your friends the tiniest bit . . . *disappointed*? You knew them in college, or before. They were excited, and stylish, and adroit. They moved easily. They were comfortable in the world. (If your friends were rich, they are still comfortable in the world, but tend to associate more with other rich people as they get older. It turns out that college is the last place in the world where money really didn't matter quite so much.) Do they seem comfortable now? Do they seem to be where they thought they would be at age twenty-five, or at age thirty?

Didn't we imagine we'd have money, and houses, and families of our own, as we approached the end of our twenties? Didn't we imagine we'd be easy in our lives—that life would be an affair of lawns and washed cars and coming in through the front door of our own houses? If we live in cities, we knew our friends in their first apartments. We knew them sharing one-bedrooms with sofa beds, but with a cheerful sense that this was temporary and, because it was temporary, *interesting*. We'd had our freshman years in high school and college. Now we were having our freshman years in the world. It was going to be interesting to spend our first few years as adults in a little bit of a money drama. It was authentic—the big game, finally.

In those postcollege years, we still had our old wardrobes from school. Did you watch those same clothes recirculate through your friends' closets? In those first years, we still had our credit cards from college—Citibank, First Boston, and First Card had the same fantasies about our earning power, apparently, as we all did. Did you watch your friends making scrambling calls home when a bill for the card was due, for fear they would lose it? Did you begin getting calls from creditors—the college loan people, who after all *had* been patient. Did you begin getting letters from American Express that start out chummy ("You are a valued customer") but end up signed by anonymous men, by men without first names but only first initials? When you come home in the evening, and there is a message with a faraway sound on your answering machine that doesn't even give a name anymore but only an eight-hundred number, does your chest sink a little, and do you call that number back?

For there hasn't been that much change since college. We watched it happen without really noticing it, and anyway most shifts only become clear in retrospect, after they are over. The moment for getting our own apartments seemed to recede somewhere into the future. When you run into friends, they are still sleeping on sofa beds, and still wearing clothes from college. Money borrowed from our parents, grandparents, or those successful older siblings to meet panicked bills was never paid back, and our parents could tell, when we called, just by our voices, when we were going to ask for more. Now we are in our twenties—and we are still freshmen in the world, to a degree. The fantasy version of ourselves continues to live in a charming apartment somewhere else, or is married in a house with a car outside. That fantasy vision is waiting for us to join it. It wonders why we are late. It wonders if we are ever coming.

Americans never admit disappointment. In a novel called *Dog Soldiers,* Robert Stone writes of how far people went out of their way, in Vietnam, not to seem unlucky. It was unsafe to appear so. "Unlucky-looking people made the Vietnamese uneasy and even tempted some to assume the role of misfortune. . . . It was necessary to appear as though innate good fortune made one invulnerable." In America, if you are having a difficult time, it is hard to do anything except continue to have a difficult time. People can smell it on you. No one likes relying on something that isn't a sure thing. Friends, family, can be wonderfully supportive, but eventually they wonder when the story will change. We talked about this already, didn't we? Last year? So why are we still talking about it? Why is *this* still on? We want to be successful and entertaining, in America. If you aren't successful, it is very hard to become so. Ask someone if they are *disappointed* and you are not likely to get any answer at all. But most of us are not where we intended to be.

Martin Amis wrote about this in 1978, in a novel with the ironic title *Success.* The narrator is a young man finding his postgraduate way in London.

I worry about money all the time. I daren't open letters any more. I haven't bought any new clothes since March . . . (and most of my clothes are ridiculous—I can't wear them to work). Buying anything non-essential makes me feel furtive, criminal, a counterfeiter. Damn it, *any* exchange of money for goods fills me with inordinate fear. Inordinate? I cannot live on the money I am paid. Nobody could. I cannot get to and from work every day and eat and not quite go mad. I cannot *stay alive* on what I earn. . . . I can no longer read a book or even watch television without this other drama rearing up inside my mind, mangling page and screen. I cannot do anything without money leering over my shoulder. I think about money all the time. Money has robbed me of everything I had.

It is hard to explain what happened—although something clearly *did* happen. The parents we talk to will take two tacks. The tacks they take depend on the point they want to make, but when you consider them they are mutually exclusive. They disqualify each other, because they can't both be true, at least not at the same time. The first tack is the most painful one, the one we joke about with our friends: Our parents say, "By the time I was your age, I was married, I had a job, I understood about commitment and responsibility." This generally means our parents don't think we are trying effectively to get jobs or find spouses; these are the words we hear when we borrow money, the service charge we must pay to get it. The second tack is: Our parents say, "Things aren't any harder now than when we were young. We knew how to live cheaply." But if things *weren't* harder, why were they able to buy houses and risk marriages? The two statements must be combined: If they were our age now, in 1994, would they be married or moving in careers or qualifying for mortgages? One young woman explained to us, talking about her own parents, "My mother and father wouldn't last ten minutes if they were my age now."

Stephen Gleick, a man who graduated from college in the late eighties, attended a Christmas party in 1992 as the last-minute date of a woman he did not know well. The party was held in an apartment much larger and more well-appointed than his own—the kind of apartment he had imagined for himself in his late twenties. It was very formal—the people hosting the party were playing at being adults. Stephen told us he did not want to talk with anyone, that when inevitable questions of what he was doing were raised, he answered them as quickly as he could and tried to shift to some other topic. After dinner, the couples moved into the living room, with drinks and music. Most of the people came from rich families, and were a few years older than he was. Many were married. "It was as if only people with money could afford to grow up," Stephen said. One woman, whom he had known at college, had married an older man from France, and Steve was astonished at the difference between her position and his. The party was friendly, but there was a sense of unreality to the event—the men, just off work, were wearing suits, while Stephen was in the clothes he'd worn all day. These people were only a little older than him but were living in a world completely different than his own. He felt *displaced*. It was the kind of party he had enjoyed attending in college, and when he talked about it, he finally said, "I felt like I was attending the party of some people I used to be like. And there they all were, mature and married, and I was a *curiosity* to them, in a sense. I felt like they really were adults, and there I was and I wasn't quite one of them."

We all know where we wanted to be at this age. We were all raised in the America where TV families live very well—or even if they are living badly, nothing disastrous happens, or the cast would have to disband, and the show would be over. Weekly television is based on this idea of changelessness, of nothing being unresolvable—but in real life when there is a bill to pay, we can't wait till the end of the half hour to pay it.

The adult life we aspired to, finally, is one based on having money. Nothing remarkable about that. It doesn't need to be a lot of money. Many of us felt perversely happy when the stock market crashed in 1987—we thought it would throw a curve to people for whom everything seemed to have come too easily. We remember almost an exhilaration—this horrible thing was happening, but it was happening to someone else. Now it has somehow happened to us: The country we have lived in since 1987 has been one of scarcity, in which the goals we set for ourselves have become more and more difficult to realize, and where if we stop to ask ourselves what is delaying us, it always comes down to money. Money has prevented us from fully separating from our parents. Money has prevented us from marrying and starting families at the age when many of us would have preferred being married and parents. Money has kept us living with roommates, living at home, borrowing from each other. Money has kept us where we were, where we are. Other problems have solutions: You can call the lover you fought with and reconcile with them; you can decide to read more, or watch TV less, or eat less and exercise more, or quit smoking or take up smoking, or start dancing or stop dancing so often. But if money is your stumbling block, there is no way to think or talk your way out of it.

In a 1987 collection, the writer John Updike refers to his own early adulthood, in the story "The Lovely Troubled Daughters of Our Old Crowd." He writes of the young newlyweds his narrator lived among in the early sixties—and it is this life, of course, to which we aspire. The life of easy socializing, of progress of some kind. Updike has always had an acute ear for social change; he writes of the children of his old friends, in the late eighties, who don't seem to be enjoying their youth effectively. They have moved back in with their parents. They work day jobs as secretaries or in gift shops, and seem, to the narrator, morose and under-animated. Updike asks, "These women: What are they hanging back for? What are they afraid of?" Because of Updike's preoccupations, he hints that the blame for this pause is in his narrator's old adulteries. But there is another reason. In the story, reminiscing about his own late twenties, he writes, "We were in our late twenties then, young at being old—the best of times."

We have become the opposite. Old at being young.

When you're young, you run not on achievement but on promise. Promise is the lure of youth—this person is so "well spoken" for her age, this person is so "knowledgeable, smooth, stylish" for his age. When they are full adults—boy, *that* will be something!

But when you enter your mid-twenties, your late twenties, your early thirties, the scoring method shifts. Now achievements are the only thing that matter. They are what you have to show for yourself with friends, ex-lovers, parents, employers. Promise is gone. And if your achievements aren't there, all you can do is avoid the question, or joke sickeningly, and remember when you were promising. To face your middle twenties in the position of adolescence—all promise and no achievement, other than being older—is a dismal prospect. People wonder why you are a late bloomer. They wonder if you will bloom at all. One college graduate told *The Wall Street Journal,* in the summer of 1993, that when she considered her life in Portland, baby-sitting or taking temp jobs, engaging in a lot of gallows humor with her similarly underemployed friends, there was one thing she missed. Said this woman, "I miss the old me."

Late bloomers' disappointment is headquartered here. We are not happy to be playing the adolescent role anymore. Our lives still exist somewhere ahead of us. We watch the idyllic commercials on television, of couples moving in and out of focus, enjoying the freedom that only a good, low-priced chardonnay from California can bring. They are reveling in the pleasure of a new convertible automobile. They are married, or stable—they don't seem to be constantly measuring each other, for flaws and inadequacies. They have jobs—or else how could they afford the new auto, which has made such a lovely difference in their lives? They are free from grinding care, from personal accountancy. They have their own homes. They entertain there. They are stable and social—they need a reliable California white. This is what America wants us to want, and we do. That freedom from money-worry; that ease. That life, the ease that comes from finding a space in it in which to live.

America has always placed its bets on youth. Other generations have panicked about losing their youth—Marshall Herskovitz, who was the great fresco-painter of his baby-boom generation with just the opening credits to *thirtysomething,* referred to his generation as "the generation that never wanted to grow up." Most of the people our own age we spoke to have wanted *only* to grow up. That is the position so many of us are in—longing for the time when life will feel routine, and settled, and adult.

This book is about those of us who are still waiting—the late bloomers. Why so many of us feel old at being young. Why we are still waiting for the momentous *something* that will transform our lives. We want to turn our attention to the smaller questions (what wine, which car, what way to spend the weekend). We are waiting for life to cease being an affair of jury-rigged solutions to sudden problems. We are waiting for choices to cease being matters of expedience. We have been waiting for a long time—waiting to bloom, waiting to replace promise with achievement. This book will try to explain why and how this has come to be.

# i.
# reporting a
# generation

"What do they expect? You hear things like, 'These kids—they don't care about anything, they're apathetic.' But you try caring about acid rain or the environment. Until you have acid rain falling on your head, it's hard to care. It was easy to care about Vietnam: People were going to die. I'm always baffled—what is it that they want? Do they wish we were in a war, so we could show our heart was in the right place by protesting it?"

—Jennifer Davies, Los Angeles, California, twenty-four

i.

## "for the twentysomething crowd . . .
## second best seems just fine."
—Time, *July 1990*

What do we know about ourselves from the media? There are certain facts about people our age. The age for first marriage is higher than it has ever been since the United States began taking a yearly census of itself in 1890. (It is twenty-seven for men, a little under twenty-five for women.) We know that rooming with our parents is the most common living arrangement for those of us under twenty-five. (Three out of five of these people you meet are still living with their parents. Even for those of us over thirty, one quarter still share an address with their folks.) If we read the news magazines and watch TV, we find that one third of us are unemployed (ABC News broadcast this number in 1992), and that our incomes have dropped 20 percent in the last twenty years—that in 1973, as we sort of guessed, the average twenty-five-year-old was earning a good deal more money each year than he was in 1993. We also find that living expenses have grown at an inverse and even speedier rate—that it now costs 50 percent more to rent an apartment than it did even ten years ago. These are the hard numbers.

What do we know about ourselves as *people,* as a generation with certain definable shared tastes and attitudes?

This comes to us from the same sources. We may have a dim memory of how we were portrayed in the mid- to late eighties. And we may even have the sense that something *shifted* in this decade. But it's hard to put our fingers on it, on when the shift occurred, or on how the new information arrived. People look at us differently than they once did. It's always "Yes, but" when it comes to us. They look at us with . . . *reservations.*

How *do* those who are ahead see us? "I think almost everybody I know feels that your generation is growing up very slowly," Natalie Norvick, a fifty-year-old mother, explained. "It's on the slow path. With work and social relations. With willingness and interest in assuming responsibility—in working hard and being somewhat self-sufficient. I feel there's a lack of commitment. Looking down on getting married and having children." Arthur Ryan, a father, said, "There's an impression that a lot of people your age don't forge ahead. That you aren't dedicated, that you don't want to pay dues. When we got out of school, we would take any job. You'll only take jobs you *like.*" The head of a Cincinnati ad agency said he had the sense that "young people today aren't working as hard." Though when the parents were asked about their own children, they offered extenuating circumstances—one kid *was* married, two kids had advanced degrees (MBA and social work) and had not been able to find jobs in their fields and had *then* gone on to make up their own jobs. The Cincinnati adman, asked about his own twentysomething employees, admitted that they were able to commit to projects, and would stay at the office as long as those projects required. It was as if these people knew there was some national impression of what our generation was like, and had to find excuses for why the experiences of the twentysomethings they knew well didn't quite match it. It was as though they had a very clear idea of what their answer was *supposed* to be—and were puzzled and willing to trust that answer more than their own observations.

If you look at TV reports about late bloomers, or read magazine stories about people our age, you see where the impression arises. The journalist Susan Faludi once compared the national media to a game of Telephone. She's right, in a sense. An image gets picked up, kicked around, added to and subtracted from, inflated and distorted, until finally it's run the length of the country and is very far from the perhaps simple notions that first created it.

The image the country has of us is a group of young people wearing Doc Martens, avoiding work, avoiding marriage, wearing nose rings, and speaking an emphatic kind of White Suburban Jive—"Dude," "Like," "Hel-*lo!*" et cetera. If you close your eyes and imagine the average "twentysomething," it would come out something like this: scruffy-haired, devoted to Soundgarden, undependable and uninterested in jobs, a slave to television, disengaged from news and politics, unable to consider or even to construct an argument. And yet—happy. Perversely, unwaveringly happy. Spicolli played this role in 1984, in *Fast Times at Ridgemont High,* from Cameron Crowe's book of the same name. John Cusack played it with variations in 1987's *Say Anything* (written and directed by Cameron Crowe). In 1992, Matt Dillon played the exact same role in *Singles* (a product of the same Cameron Crowe). There is something comic and puppyish about the flustered, clumsy attempts of this young person to engage with the

17

real, hard machinery of the actual world. When we imagine ourselves through the eyes of the media, we are the kids wearing play clothes, ripped jeans and waist-tied flannel shirts. We have play haircuts. You can't imagine what our source of income is, though the suspicion is that it is probably some more diligent and dedicated family member. In ads directed at young people—Panasonic and Sony's electronics spots, Pepsi's Mountain Dew ad, Ford's Mustang come-on— we are not adults but people deliberately at recess. The Subaru that tried to sell itself this way was so irritating that on the computer bulletin board GenX, one user asked, "Anyone see the 'Gen-X' Subaru commercial? You know, the one with the 'grunge' clothes spewing some BS about how Subarus are like punk rock? Does anyone else wanna kill this guy?" A score of affirmative responses followed. The image we get from the media is one of *happiness*—the fool in *King Lear,* having a great time while Lear wanders the heath. Everyone else is working, but this kid is out there in the sun, wearing a Walkman and climbing mountains. Happy life on the margins.

The alternate image is of the gloomy preadult, wearing black, who writes and reads 'zines, works at Domino's or some job like that, and frets over the bad hand dealt to him. A scoffer at the values of the culture—a nineties punk, but of course too sophisticated to fully embrace that ethic. A stern-eyed, PC disliker of the country. We get to be Puck, or we get to be Caliban. In both cases, the person presented wouldn't be *unhappy* not to be adult yet—just the opposite. This person will be happy as long as their money-source holds out. Into their thirties, into their forties. Still working at Domino's; still talking in White Suburban Jive. Maybe reading Ayn Rand, but still out there trying to have fun. Certainly, this is not someone an employer would want to hire. It is not someone an intelligent and careful man or woman would want to marry. It is someone who finds their engagement in sensation and not in achievement. It is a marketing construct, to an extent—if we find our pleasure in sensation, it means that pleasure will come from watching TV and from buying the products promoted there, so it fits the needs of advertisers nicely. It is an undependable person—so, in a sense, it fits the needs of those who don't want to make any new hiring of young people, and yet also don't want to address what this tells them about the direction of the country. But these groups didn't create the image. Where did it come from?

Here's how Neil Howe and William Strauss described people our age in a long December 1992 cover story of *The Atlantic:*

> As they shield their eyes with Ray-Ban Wayfarer sunglasses, and their ears with Model TCD-D3 Sony Walkman, today's teens and twentysomethings present to Boomer eyes a splintered image of brassy looks and smooth manner, [of] kids more comfortable shopping or playing than working or studying . . . They watch too much TV, seldom vote, cheat on tests, don't read newspapers.

And from a very different part of the country, serving a very different constituency, in an April 1993 article in *The Houston Chronicle:* "Baby boomers see twentysomethings as poorly educated, politically apathetic, morally obtuse grunge rockers who spend their time eating junk food and watching MTV."

How did *this* come to be our image? When Faludi said the media was like a game of Telephone, she meant that a newspaper or magazine story is a guess about which way the culture is heading. Other magazines, seeing a new topic to be covered, will publish their own stories, assessing that guess. Because television news shows are voracious—they must fill their programming menu night after night, week after week, they're always on the prowl—they are intrigued by fresh information. A "new" way of looking at things is always a good bet, and a "new attitude" is even better. So they will report in good faith the stories from these magazines. Finally, television and movies—themselves on the lookout for a new story, for an untapped plotline—will take the version of this guess that has already appeared on TV and in newspapers (it *must* be true), and turn it into entertainment. That's the final stop—the circle has been run, and an image has been fixed. Look at the character Joey, for example, on the NBC series *Blossom.* Look at the story lines on *Melrose Place.* Or look at the copy for the short-lived ABC series *Home Free,* about a young man returning to his parents: "He Came. He Saw. He Moved Back In." A guess is reported, repeated, and finally returned to the country as truth, because it has proved itself by appearing in so many venues.


## ii.
## "proceeding with caution"
### —Time, *July 1990*


What has the press written about young people in the workplace?

*Business Week* pointed out that "job attitudes are veering from the old work ethic." The magazine quoted a disappointed supervisor who did not like the employees who were starting to show up at his office. "People here aren't what they used to be," this man said. "Several years ago, most of our employees had good values. They were ambitious, conscientious, hard-working, and honest, and you could count on them to get the job done. Now we're getting some different types who are difficult to supervise." The magazine reported that these different-type young people "shunned work which ties them down." They were going to be "difficult to supervise" because you could no longer count on money as your motivating factor. Instead, setting goals and solving problems had become "more important than the money or the prestige associated with the position."

*U.S. News & World Report* had similar observations to make about young people. "The activities of the generation as a whole remain considerably different from those of their parents in such matters as sex, family life, attitudes toward work, politics, and so on." The magazine worried about the generation's "tentative sexual relationships," about young adults who were "destabilizing the basic unit of society—the nuclear family—to an enormous degree." The magazine feared that national affluence had given young adults "too much, too soon." One sociologist suggested, "This makes them different from preceding generations. Because they were born in a period when all groups of society were acquiring an unprecedented amount of goods and affluence, they have been less attracted by money and work. Money is less important. It's there to be spent, but it's not worth making sacrifices for." The *U.S. News* article worried about the large number of young people who were moving back into their parents' homes. The magazine spoke of a "rejection of material goods" and pointed out that "for this generation, the age of heroes is dead. . . . [T]hey may never find leaders to look up to the way many people did before." *U.S. News* spoke of the problem of political apathy and found, "For many young people, the pursuit of happiness is the dominant preoccupation."

These criticisms sound glumly, fascinatingly familiar—but the two articles they are taken from appeared in 1975 and 1978. *Business Week*'s piece was published during the jittery depths of the oil shock, when inflation was considered a great threat to the national well-being. The *U.S. News* article appeared three years after that. Both articles were about *baby boomers,* and yet we know these people turned out to be okay, the "ultimate workaholics"—the same workaholics now criticizing us for our lassitude.

What makes the claims so familiar is that the same criticisms were made about people in their twenties again, one month into the 1990 recession, by *Time* magazine. *Time*'s July cover story released an image of us to the culture, and reported its findings as though they were something unprecedented. It was the *Time* article that cobbled together our age and a television program and gave us the unlovely phrase "twentysomething." And it was in the *Time* article that we were first pegged as "whiners"—this stuck, to the point where whenever any late bloomer observes, in the most measured, calm, somber and serious tone, "I am surprised and grieved by the unfortunate way America's economic life has turned out," someone is there to say, "Quit your whining, pal."

The *Time* article was called "Proceeding with Caution," and the subtitle said everything. "The twentysomething generation is balking at work, marriage and baby-boomer values. Why are today's young adults so skeptical?"

There were ten sections, which were intended to introduce young people to the readers of *Time*. On the cover, six people our age—all in black, all looking slightly malnourished—stare away from the camera. It was not the most smashing way to be introduced. In each of the sections—about culture, about marriage, about politics—the achievements and aims of our generation were made to seem small and insubstantial. We were classified as "paralyzed," as "shirkers." The criticisms sounded very much like the ones in the articles from the mid-seventies, about the *previous* generation of young adults.

In "Leaders: Heroes Are Hard to Find": "Young adults need role models and leaders, but the twentysomething generation has almost no one to look up to"—the exact observation *U.S. News* made in 1978.

In "Dating: Don't Stand So Close": "Finding a mate is a challenge for a generation that has elevated casual commitment to an art form"—and once again, this echoed the remarks about "tentativeness" in forming relationships and starting marriages from the article more than a decade earlier.

In "Careers: Not Just Yet, Thanks": "Crass materialism is on the wane"—just as the *U.S. News* article claimed. "Most of all, young workers want job gratification"—just as the 1975 *Business Week* article had it. "[Twentysomethings] want short term tasks with observable results," complained a New York ad agent (cf. *Business Week*). "This generation refuses to pay its dues," added a marketer (cf. *U.S. News*). Combining this statement with *Time*'s 1990 suggestion that "the young work force is considered overly sensitive at best and lazy at worst," throwing in the article's claim that "while recruiters are trying to woo young workers, a generation is out planning its escape from the 9-to-5 routine," and we arrive back with *Business Week* in 1975, with their fear that the work ethic had disappeared from young people in America.

We know what American values are supposed to be.

Confident, driven, success-oriented. These were no longer the values of young people, according to the "twentysomething" cover story. Said *Time,* "They have trouble making decisions." Said *Time,* "They are seeking an escape from Western culture, rather than further refinement to smooth their entry into society." Said *Time,* "The leitmotiv for the new age: Second place seems just fine."

Worried *U.S. News* in 1978: "The activities of the generation as a whole remain considerably different from those of their parents" in sex, family life, work, and politics. Worried *Time* in 1990: "Anyone who expected they would echo the boomers who came before, bringing more of the same attitude, should brace for a surprise. This crowd is profoundly different from—even contrary to—that group." And *Time,* in its ten sections, showed just how different those views were—in sex, family life, work, and politics.

We're not noting the similarities for the pleasures of coincidence. The coincidence points to something else. Articles like these tend to get written at periods of national unease. The seventies articles were written about the baby boom, but it was the baby boom as it existed just after the Vietnam pullout and just before the Carter "malaise." The *Time* article was written in the first uneasy month of the 1990 recession. In her 1989 book *Fear of Falling,* the journalist Barbara Ehrenreich made a deadly accurate point about American values. In times of economic crisis, the middle class looks to character for "explanations." It tends to project its concerns onto others—and what the middle class projects onto others, Ehrenreich wrote, is "what the middle class fears most in itself. A softening of character, a lack of firm inner values." When things get tough economically, Americans begin to look for some trouble in the national psyche, some quirk that is making what has been a successful country *un*successful. In the middle of the seventies recession, American journalists had turned to the then-young baby boom, and found in that generation the root of the problem. They were soft. They lacked the values of hard work and ambition on which America thrived. Similarly, in the 1990 recession, magazine writers were startled by the changes that were beginning to move through the country. They turned to us, as they had turned to young people fifteen years earlier, to give those problems a face. They did not like the face they saw there. What was confusing for us as a generation was that for five years before that, we had been reading very different things about ourselves. We had been focused on and examined as the emblem for a whole different range of problems.

iii.
## "I returned thinking that young people are older than they used to be."
—*Bruce Weber, in* The New York Times Magazine, *April 1987*

There had been any number of essays and editorials about the baby bust in the years before 1990. They simply sprang from a very different set of anxieties. During the eighties, the fear was that young people were growing up too quickly. Young people were far *too* driven. Young people were the dead-souled, cold-eyed pioneers of a new America, an America concerned solely with success.

We're talking of course about feature articles—what Susan Faludi called "trend" stories. News stories—containing hard data, of employment rates and census results—do not tend to have an opinion. They are presentations of numbers and events. Trend stories are something else. They are longer articles. They are guesses. They are ways the nation takes its own pulse, gathers data about itself, and tries to make predictions about where it is going. In a sense, they are bedtime stories journalists prepare to try to soothe and address fears the country may have been experiencing in this month or that one. In her 1991 book *Backlash,* Faludi defined the "trend" story by three things: its absence of data, its generalizations, and its reliance on words like "increasingly" and "more and more." In Faludi's opinion, trend stories do not contain "news" but the journalists' anxieties about where the culture is headed. As Faludi put it, these stories prescribe more often than they predict or observe.

It is very easy for journalists to write trend stories about the young, because the young are, in a sense, the clearest image of the culture's values. They haven't had enough ideas of their own yet to compare and contrast with what the culture is giving them. They are undented by experience, so they give the truest reflection.

The worry about the country during the 1980s was that we had *all* become too concerned with money and getting ahead. This was an era, after all, in which magazines ran articles like "Getting By on One Million a Year," when journalists worried about the nation's fixation on money. And so articles about young people reflected these concerns. It was a way for journalists to examine those values in a neutral way. *We* were the ones too worried about success and getting ahead. Was this a good thing, or a bad thing? The worry about people our age in the years leading up to 1990 was that we were *too* single-minded, *too* careerist. That we had no values at all, save for achieving our own ends.

Paul Johnson, for example, wrote a long essay in *The*

*New York Times* in 1984, speaking of "the harsh, dry, materialistic wind" that was then sweeping across college campuses. What he called the New Materialism could be found primarily among people in their late teens and early twenties. To Johnson, it was unquestionably a widespread phenomenon. Success, dedication, and determination were all being "glamorized." The author wrote that a student at Princeton had told him, in a comic reversal of what many imagined were the priorities of youth, "People here are interested in jobs and sex. In that order." Johnson called his article "The Lost Ideals of Youth."

The novelist David Leavitt was probably the first writer of our age to make any impression on the general culture. In a long *Esquire* essay in 1985, Leavitt wrote that we had turned our backs on politics, activism, and idealism. He wrote of his own shudder of distaste when passing a candlelit vigil on his Yale campus. This distaste was based, Leavitt confessed, on *fashion*—it no longer made sense to be concerned with politics, it was out of date, the country had changed in ways so as to make student protest more an exercise of benign nostalgia than a legitimate pursuit. Instead, according to Leavitt, our generation was interested in economic security and the promise of comfort. After years of financial turbulence and domestic surprises, our generation had sharpened its focus. As Leavitt put it, "We trust ourselves, and money. Period." Leavitt's piece—and Leavitt was twenty-eight the year the "twentysomething" story was published—did not give the impression of a generation balking at adulthood. Just the opposite. "For people in my generation," he wrote, "the goal seems to be to get to thirty as fast as possible, and stay there." He spoke of a pragmatic group that was somewhat defiantly proud to have no values; he wrote of the detached, ironic voice of our generation, which was forever assuring itself, At least you're not faking it, as they did; at least you're not pretending, as they did. His piece reiterated, in first person, the points Paul Johnson had made in the *Times* a year earlier. Said Leavitt, "We are interested in stability, neatness, entrenchment. We want to stay in one place and in one piece, establish careers, establish credit. We want good apartments, fulfilling jobs, nice boy/girl friends. We want American Express Gold Cards." It was not of course the most salutary statement—and this was part of Leavitt's irony. This was part of his point. As Leavitt said, at least our generation wasn't going to fake it, at least our generation wasn't going to pretend it had private values it wasn't putting into practice. What was the point of paying polite lip service to politics and ideals when we all secretly agreed that the good things in life—homes, relationships—were derived from money?

The same year, *Fortune* magazine—a Time-Life publication—published its own article on the first wave of our generation: "The Baby Bust Hits the Job Market." *Fortune* published this kind of article every ten years, so that readers and employers might know what to expect from the "freshly minted" adults heading into the real world.

As *Fortune*'s editor wrote, "The reporters were astounded by their fierce competition and resourcefulness." Like the people Leavitt and Johnson wrote about, the students interviewed seemed *old* to the reporters. They were "nail-biters and champion worrywarts," doing whatever they thought it took to secure themselves employment. *Fortune* wrote of the "competitive frenzy" to find jobs. One twenty-two-year-old, commenting on what she had seen of the national life, said, "I don't ever want to be in a position where I can't do the things I want to do because of money." Another twenty-two-year-old told the magazine, "It would be nice to be able to be a kid for a few more years. But I'm not counting on it." What *Fortune* missed in these students was some of the *ease* of youth, the freedom from adult anxiety, which established adults especially prize in the young. (The young, who see the glories and plot-twists of adult life every evening on television, are mostly interested in getting on with it.) As the magazine put it, addressing a very different worry than the ones that would be addressed again and again in the nineties, "With all the worrying the class of '85 is doing, it's tempting, to roll the eyes and mutter something about kids today."

The novelist Bret Easton Ellis wrote of similar value changes he saw on his own Bennington campus. Bennington is supposed to be a school for artists—for those *not* interested in "getting ahead." But even at Bennington, as Ellis wrote in *Rolling Stone* in 1986, a new attitude had arrived. "There is a lot of talk about college students 'cleaning up their act' and becoming more responsible and work-oriented, and they are." Yet he worried that, "with their seriousness about making money and their fear of failure," kids were turning "robotic." What troubled Ellis was not a turning away from all values, but a too *strenuous,* too grasping and immediate embrace of what we all would recognize as American aims, the values of success-orientation and comfort. To Ellis, this constituted a turning away from all that he considered commendable in America. Our generation was being sucked in by the American success myth and was becoming "weird." Wrote Ellis, "Something, however unidentifiable it is, has happened."

So it went throughout the decade. Anxieties about our generation's values expressed by members of the generation, and then anxieties expressed by writers *outside* the generation. It is important to point out that no one thought it "wrong" to associate money with safety—growing up in the seventies would have assured that—it was simply what everyone could agree upon about young people. We were smooth and capable. In *The Washington Post,* Robert Samuelson allowing that the new materialism among the young was to be expected. In *Forbes,* a vaguely affectionate look at us as "ambitious overachievers." In 1987, in a cover story for *The New York Times Magazine,* Bruce Weber dubbing us "The Unromantic Generation." Weber wrote of traveling the country to interview sixty recent college graduates and finding them to be "without ideals and fantasies" and without what he considered to be youthful attitudes. He received a few offers for "homecooked meals," and a lot of commendation for his secure job at the *Times.* "I returned," he wrote, "thinking that young people are older than they used to be."

Weber's tone was one of fond vexation—he wondered whether young people, in their drive for success, were missing out on the good things in life: Love, the willingness to take risks, the freedom that willingness admits. These were the worries the culture had about itself in the late eighties. Was *everyone* too fixated on getting ahead? Was life becoming too regimented? It was easy to examine this in the young. Wrote Weber, of his many interviews, "A quality emerged, to a degree that I'd call it characteristic. They are planners. They look ahead with certainty. They have priorities. I'd ask about love, they'd give me a graph." Weber did not find our generation "soulless," as Ellis had found us, but "determined." We were "career-minded, fiercely self-reliant." Weber's conclusions were the opposite of what *Time* would report three years later—yet they were very much in line with what these other observers had been saying. His subjects had their professional success in mind first; they had accomplishment in mind first. Weber felt his own generation had not been as single-minded. As Weber wrote, "The theme of getting on track and staying there surfaced again and again. I came to think of it as the currency of self-definition."

In June of 1989, one year before the "twentysomething" cover story, *Fortune* ran a second long article about the generation. This was one of the last articles of its kind to be written before the recession, which started in July of 1990. *Fortune* reiterated many of the observations that it had made in 1985. "These young men and women are confident, ambitious, and smart," said the article's author. Where *Time* would write one year later—of the exact same generation— that twentysomethings would be a tough sell to the business world, that they wanted to "escape" the nine-to-five grind, *Fortune* had quite different findings. "Seldom have the personal attitudes of a graduating class meshed so neatly with the needs of business."

Almost every finding of the article was the reverse of the article that would be written one year later. No materialism? "To be sure," wrote *Fortune,* "the graduates are not exactly indifferent to the green stuff." The official T-shirt for the Harvard class of 1989 had the motto "Going for the Gold"— and on the back of that T-shirt, as punchline, was a big American Express Gold Card. (This, of course, was the same joke Leavitt had made in 1985.) Wrote *Fortune,* "The apparent greediness of many a student may be a reaction to the enormous financial burden of a college education. . . . College seniors owe an estimated $10 billion in school loans, and the discipline of debt is doing for graduates exactly what it is supposed to do for corporations—it focuses attention on the business at hand." As Ernest Boyer, president of Carnegie Foundation for the Advancement of Teaching, told the magazine, the work ethic was very strong among twentysomethings. "Employers will be dealing with young people who want to work."

31

And rather than just being backed up by their article-by-article repetition, the opinions and findings of those authors and magazines were supported by the numbers. National studies of college course enrollment showed a steady gain for the business major, doubling from 12 percent of all degrees in 1970 to 25 percent in 1985. This growth came at the expense of other, less marketable disciplines. Humanities majors—which seemed to guarantee the worst job prospects—had dropped from 50 percent of all degrees to 30 percent in the same fifteen years. UCLA's Higher Education Research Institute, which polls the attitudes of the nation's incoming freshmen, found a similar change in attitudes. Our generation had become *more* career-conscious, *more* money-oriented, with every year. In 1966, 84 percent of all incoming freshmen had reported that "Developing a Meaningful Philosophy of Life" was their most important goal; only 44 percent felt that "Being Very Well Off Financially" was most important. But by 1990, these proportions had reversed. Only 37 percent now felt that a "Meaningful philosophy" was the most important life goal; 76 percent now answered that "Financial success" was their primary aim. Nor did these attitudes change after four years of schooling. Among seniors, the proportions were even higher. According to Roper CollegeTrack—a national firm for accumulating information on graduates—93 percent of 1989's college seniors listed "Financial security" as their major life goal. Three quarters of them answered that future career success had been the most important factor in selecting their universities. Said *Time* in 1990, "They would rather hike in the Himalayas than climb a corporate ladder." Said Stuart Himmelfarb, president of CollegeTrack, in 1989, "These young people have bought into the process."

Is there any way to account for a sea change in the attitude of our generation in just twelve months? Or is it easier to account for a sea change in the *coverage* of that attitude? Certainly, the evidence would tend to steer one in the second direction. After all, the proportion of students in the HERI studies becoming career-oriented had been steadily climbing for more than a decade. The testimony of young writers like Leavitt and Ellis inclines one to that belief, as does the testimony of older journalists like Weber and the editors at *Fortune*. So one would have to argue that there had been no basic change in mindset. That by 1990, we could agree on certain basic statements about ourselves: We had staked our personal futures on being *capable*; that we meant to become established as quickly as possible. So there was no large-scale shift in our generation's goals. Instead, something in the culture changed between 1989 and 1990.

iv.

"I think it would be nice
if there was an acknowledgment
that people in their twenties
can really actually get up
and *do* something
without being told
or hand-held to do it.
that would be an accomplishment."

—*Two twenty-four-year-olds on ABC's*
*"Twentysomething: What Happened to the*
*American Dream?," July 1992*

What happened was the recession, which started in July of 1990. The market for postgraduate jobs had begun softening as early as 1989—this is the subject of Chapter 2—but the actual recession didn't strike the country as a whole until the following year.

The recession was particularly difficult for us. It was a "white-collar" recession, which meant it tended to affect college graduates more powerfully than other groups. (This isn't to say it didn't affect non–college graduates, only that they had been pushed to the side in the *previous* recession.) And this was a white-collar recession with a difference. During the first twelve months of the recession, 1.45 million jobs were lost to the country, and twentysomethings accounted for 65 percent of the job losses. Since twentysomethings make up less than one fifth of the workforce, this meant they had suffered four times more pain during that first year than any other group. A 1992 study by the Children's Defense Fund put the numbers slightly higher. There were one million fewer twentysomethings on the job in May of 1991 than there had been in May of 1990. This was probably the last-hired, first-fired principle, as one might have predicted—but the result was a lot of us out of work, a painful reality regardless of the cause.

The recession had been coming for a long while. Although the stock crash in 1987 didn't immediately affect the country, it was the first sign, and it sent out nervous little ripples. The weakness it revealed became more apparent as that decade drew to a close. According to the political writer William Greider, both presidential candidates in 1988 knew a recession would have to come in the early nineties—as a corrective—although neither talked about it in their campaign platforms or speeches. The country had gotten *shakier*. Bush gave the impression of being perpetually out of town—of being a kind of absentee landlord—and he lacked Reagan's gift for mimicking the opportunistic murmur of our hopes. The national debt had grown unnervingly high.

In the 1980s, American journalists had projected their fears about what success would mean for the country onto young people. Were we becoming a nation of the soulless, driven only by economic and material passions? So, in the 1990s, American journalists began to project their fears about what failure might mean for the country onto young people. As Ehrenreich had written, the spiritual life of Americans is characterized by "insecurity and anxiety," by the fear of "inner weakness, of growing soft, of failing to strive, of losing discipline and will." When the country officially entered recession in July of 1990, it was these exact fears that were projected onto this generation. This was the image of our generation that began to stick.

The last "old values" article about us appeared in the magazine *American Demographics* in April of 1990. The magazine's editor found young people to be more interested in financial and professional advancement than ever—and concluded by saying, "The baby busters are activists looking out for their own interests. If you're standing in their way, look out." This was perhaps the final time that the image of a determined and independent generation would appear in a major journalistic medium. *Time,* instead set the terms for the new vision of young people, a vision reflecting new anxieties about America. It replaced the image that had reigned for six years, of driven and adaptable young people, with the image of a "confused," "paralyzed," "indecisive," and "reluctant" generation.

As we have discussed, the story had three basic points: Young people in America didn't want to work, didn't want to marry, and didn't want to become adults. In this, we were "different" from other generations, from the other people with whom we shared the nation.

The new image suited the new economy very well. It was easiest to believe that if young adults weren't working, it was because they *no longer wanted to work*. To believe that the economy had shifted in such a way as to make employment very hard to come by for anyone just out of college was dispiriting, and would have required a very different set of responses by the country.

Similarly, nobody could argue that male-female relations had gotten *easier* in the past twenty years. Just look at the movies—at romantic comedies, which should now be called romantic fantasies, for the lengths the scripts must go to so we can believe in love. Richard Gere and Julia Roberts in *Pretty Woman,* Patrick Swayze and Demi Moore in *Ghost,* Demi Moore and Woody Harrelson in *Indecent Proposal.* Even Mel Gibson in 1993's *Forever Young*—he has to be frozen in ice for five decades, chased by the FBI, and airlifted to a lighthouse before he can summon up the gumption to ask his girlfriend to marry him. Or look at the opposite, the romantic terrorism movies, of which the best example was *Fatal Attraction,* which was joined by *Body Heat, Consenting Adults, 9½ Weeks, War of the Roses,* et cetera, in this subgenre. Or look at the depressing legions of pop psychology books— each with its own goofy niche to address, "foolish choices" or "reluctant men" or the simple problem of "loving too much"—stating the issue in their own mothering terms. And then there had been the huge jump in the divorce rate; and then there had been the huge jump in the domestic violence rate; and then there had been the huge jump in the sexual harassment rate; and then there had been the huge jump in the incidence of acquaintance rape. And then there was *Time,* to say of young people that they are strangely "cautious" in forming relationships—as if the magazine were being reported and printed from a lost continent of marital and consensual fidelity, in which for some reason or other people our age had capriciously chosen not to dwell.

And this was all on the soft front, on the issues of emotion and interrelations. It leaves out a decade that started with herpes (unsightly) and ended with AIDS (deadly).

Similarly, with the recession in force, workers of *all* ages were wondering whether their efforts for job and career were worthwhile. It was easy, in the mid-eighties, for the majority of Americans to feel that making work the primary focus of their lives was a worthwhile sacrifice, for those sacrifices were being repaid. People do what they are rewarded for. But with companies "downsizing," and a kind of general economic funk settling over everyone, it seemed appropriate to reconsider those decisions. We are a cause-and-effect nation—if the rewards aren't coming in, why continue to make the sacrifices? In the early nineties, for the first time, a number of national polls (of Americans of *all* ages) showed a shift away from the values of career toward the values of family and leisure. According to the Roper Poll, in 1985 the majority of employed men had seen careers as "their most important activity." By 1991, those men were in the minority: 42 percent listed "leisure" as their most important activity, and only 37 percent cited their careers. A second poll found that two thirds of all employed Americans would be willing to take salary cuts in order to have more free time for family and leisure. According to a third study, the percentage of men who would describe their job as a "career" had dropped to 48 percent, *below* majority, for the first time in a decade. These were clear changes in the national mood, worrisome changes—and yet they were applied only to members of our generation, even though polls of young adults taken throughout the decade continued to show they were among the few groups who did *not* feel this way. It was as if, with the change in the economy, and the change in social relations, young people were being taken to task for the new America, though they had taken little part in shaping it.

How much did the article affect the national impression of young people? A *Time* cover carries tremendous weight, and the article managed to set the agenda for every piece that came after it. Journalists dropped the earlier story, which they had spent six years reporting. In *The Wall Street Journal,* in *The New York Times,* in the *Chicago Tribune,* late bloomers were seen as disappointing, as people whose values were "different" and "less job-oriented" than previous generations. (*Chicago Tribune,* 1992: "Today's generation of young adults in their twenties is fueled by the 'less work' ethic.") When an article wanted to run against type, it would set out the new stereotypes and ask young people to account for them. Most articles followed type. Many were prescriptive: A long *Washington Post* piece encouraged us to "Grow Up, Crybabies." A "My Turn" in *Newsweek* called us "The Whiny Generation." These new articles began to feed off each other. If *Time* had reported a change in the attitudes of young people, it *must* be true, so reporters from other magazines went out and found the same story. Even *Fortune,* which had run articles about "fierce" and "competitive" young people twice during the preceding five years, changed the slant of it's coverage. Six weeks after the *Time* story, it abandoned its findings of one year earlier. Now the magazine asked, "What has gotten into the brains of these kids? Nothing less than a new attitude towards life and work." Forgetting what it had earlier reported, the magazine claimed that young people "refused to make sacrifices" for the sake of employers. "Their attitude: other interests—leisure, family, lifestyle, the pursuit of experience—are as important as work." It was the same charge that had been leveled against the baby boom in the mid-seventies; it was just as untrue in 1990 as it was in 1978. The magazine claimed that the simple mention of the word *materialism* was "anathema" to our generation. "Financial security, harder to come by in this age, isn't an overriding concern," the article claimed. The article of a year before—claiming that college debts and money concerns fueled most choices postgraduates made—might just as well not have been printed.

It was the Telephone game in action. The last line of the 1990 *Fortune* piece had warned prospective employers, "The most progressive ideas you'll hear from the baby busters will probably be about how they want to progress on home in good time each day." Three years later, this statement (and much else from the *Fortune* story) was echoed in a *USA Today* article with the lay-it-on-the-line title, "Busters Have a Work Ethic All Their Own": "The traditional appeals— money, prestige—have no appeal. They are much less easily motivated than people motivated by money. They want to do their job, get home and have a life."

Most of *Time*'s article, and even its strange suggestion that people our age traveled to avoid "entry into western culture," was reiterated in the 1992 book *Twentysomething: Managing and Motivating Today's New Work Force,* a study designed for hiring officers at businesses and large corporations: "They fear adulthood," "they postpone careers in favor of travel." The suggestions fanned out into other areas of the journalistic culture: *Psychology Today* now called young people "A Generation of Gripers." In a 1992 article they issued this perky warning to employers: "The twentysomethings are plentysomething to manage." Even in venues as cobwebby as the Conference Board's magazine *Across the Board,* the new definition created in 1990 could be reencountered: "They are less driven in their work habits and career planning than their predecessors. They are less willing to sacrifice family and outside interests for career advancement. They do not want to 'have it all.' "

What the Conference Board said was particularly important—this magazine, like the *New Work Force* book and the business magazines, was read by the employers who made the hiring decisions that directly affect young people's lives. As Bob Guccione, Jr.—editor and publisher of *Spin*—wrote in the *Los Angeles Times* in 1993, "The negative labels are not-so-subtle propaganda. They imply that young people regard themselves as hopeless, a doomed, lost, societally orphaned slab of history, marking time at McJobs when they bother to work at all. What right-thinking, hard-working over-thirty person would want to hire them? This helps to preserve what limited opportunities are left for people over thirty." In fact, Guccione's strong claim was borne out by the numbers. During the 1981 recession, when an entry-level job was created, it went in a majority of cases to a recent graduate. Young adults were considered cheaper to hire and easier to train. In the 1990–91 recession, this proportion was reversed. Fifty-five percent of all new job openings now went to older workers.

Part of what happened has to do with how magazine articles are written. When *Fortune,* let's say, or *Forbes,* or *U.S. News* assigns an article about twentysomethings to a reporter, that reporter goes to the magazine's library and takes out all the clippings on the subject. So once *Time*'s suppositions began to be picked up by other publications, they took on a strange veneer of truth. Of inevitability. If this has been said in so many places, it *has* to be true about young people. As one twentysomething business journalist told us, "You have to understand, these people all read each other's magazines. So if you run an article on twentysomethings, then we have to run an article on twentysomethings. And if there are enough of the same things being said, and we're on a deadline, we are going to say them too." Neil Howe and William Strauss could justly write, in their long 1992 *Atlantic* cover story, "To their elders, these young people have become a symbol of an America in decline." The wording was particularly important. We had *literally* become a symbol—but Howe and Strauss never considered just how this symbol had been constructed.

People our age found these portrayals of themselves surprising—as letters to the editors at most of these magazines suggested. They began saying they "did not want to be characterized in a generation at all." They began writing, dispiritedly, that our generation had no shared goals or drives whatsoever—thus depriving ourselves, by rejecting solidarity, of the one power we might have in changing perceptions and affecting our political lives. One young writer, in *The Washington Post,* sadly suggested that we should, as a generation, take a vote and agree to disband. In the summer of 1992, Barbara Walters hosted a special for ABC News called "Twentysomething: What Happened to the American Dream?" Walters's own copy came straight from the *Time* and *Fortune* articles: "This is a generation that pursues the quality of life. They want time for family, friends, themselves. They want to enjoy life on their own terms." Yet when she asked her panel of eight twentysomethings what their goals were, six of them gave answers that came right out of the old American playbook: They wanted career success and marriage. When Walters asked the panel what they most wanted the country to know about our generation, what was "the most important thing," the answer was immediate and unambivalent. They wanted these characterizations to stop. What should the country know about twentysomethings? "That we are responsible." What is the biggest misconception? "That we're lazy, and we don't want to work." Said two of the panelists, "I think it would be nice if there was an acknowledgment that people in their twenties can really actually get up and do something without being told or hand-held to do it. That would be an accomplishment."

In the winter of 1992, a new perception moved through the country. After a political campaign in which all three candidates agreed that the country was in need of basic repairs, a new theme entered articles about young people. We would be the ones doing the repair. Again, a consensus about the country was being shifted to fall upon young people. *U.S. News & World Report,* in its February 1993 cover story, called us the "Repair Generation." *USA Today* wrote of our strong interest in fixing up the country. By the summer of 1993, without regard to our own preferences, our "ambitions" had been shifted once again. The country felt it needed repair; it had also decided that we were the ones with the most burning desire to do that mending work.

<br>

v.

## disappointed pragmatists

Certainly, there could not have been a global shift in attitudes between 1989 and 1990. The twentysomethings we talked to—employed and unemployed—did not seem lazy and unfocused. Nor were they uninterested in materialism. They were working hard and trying to support themselves as best they could, at the same time hoping things would turn around so they could have a little more money, a little more freedom from money-anxiety. When we asked our peers, in interviews and questionnaires, if they thought we were all "lazy," their answer was an immediate "No." (One young man underlined the word three times.) The majority of them felt that young people were working *harder* now than they ever had, and there was a good reason. Most of those who had nine-to-five jobs lived in deathly fear of the same thing their older coworkers feared. That, by working lazily, they would prove themselves dispensable and be fired. Some had already been let go, in the first months of 1990 and 1991. Those who had become reemployed were not eager to repeat the experience. Some with professional degrees were indignant. "I've got an MBA, and I'm working fourteen hours a day in a machine shop," wrote one man from Chicago. "I'd like someone to come down here and tell me I'm lazy."

The disadvantages, the practical consequences, of this style of reporting can be summed up by looking at the government. During the presidential campaign, Bill Clinton wooed college audiences with a simple line: If something wasn't done, and wasn't done soon, we would become the first generation to do less well than our parents. This was his biggest applause line with people our age—the one that, heard on television, could often silence a chattering room. We rewarded Clinton with the largest margin of victory he received from any age group. Then the parade of repair articles followed in early 1993—*Washington Post, U.S. News, USA Today*. President Clinton rewarded the loyalty of gay voters by working to shift military policy. He rewarded the constancy of female voters by nominating well-qualified women to posts in the Justice Department and Supreme Court. How did he reward us? Not by continuing to speak out on the effects of the recession, and not by offering tax breaks to corporations that made a deliberate effort to hire under-thirty workers. Instead, by a program of National Service that would affect at most 250,000 of us over the next decade. Thus, we had been rewarded, and the need to consider us had passed for a time, until the *next* election cycle.

In the eighties, journalists had feared young adults would be *too* careerist; in the seventies, that they would be too unrigorous. In the sixties, they would be too rebellious. In the fifties, sociologists had blamed the then-fresh threat of nuclear war for the inability of young people to "commit" to long-term goals. The explanations vary. The fear—of young people bringing destabilizing change to the country—does not. On reflection, all these fears seem silly, just as the present fears about our generation will seem silly to people reading up on us in the next decade, the next century. In this atmosphere, it's less accurate to talk of "values" than it is to talk of moods—quirks, fads, air pockets circulating through the culture. For certainly, one could describe our mood as depressed, as a little cynical—but there's no question that, had we been adults in the early eighties, we would have been gung ho and optimistic. Had we been adults in the seventies, we'd have sunk into hot tubs and bought fat jugs of Gallo red wine. Had we been adults in the sixties, we'd have despised and agitated against the Vietnam war. Had we been adults in the fifties, we'd have been on the front lines of business, driving out to Levittown on weekends to see if we could make believe one or two of the houses looked more like "ours" than two or three of the others.

For those of us over twenty-five, we remember a time when it seemed like you *could* make good, make the culture proud, "become established," which Flaubert once described as the main goal of those under thirty. So for those of us over twenty-five, there's a humorous, wondering, and admiring attitude toward the boundlessness of our old ambition, which is counterpoint to our present, repeatedly reconfigured hopes. For those of us under twenty-five, there is a distrust of those values. There is a reluctance to admit to having wanted to marry, to having wanted a stable job, all along. To admit to having once wanted those things is to admit to being at the present moment disappointed. And no one wants to admit to disappointment. To be disappointed in America is to be shunned. We want to surround ourselves— even insulate ourselves—with upbeat people, as employees, as lovers, as friends. There is the impression that someone who is not upbeat will slow us down. Make it harder for us to get to where we want to go.

In the fall of 1993, in a *Newsweek* cover story on the new television, John Leland wrote of the viewing habits of our generation—of our particular interest in dumbed-up characters. Certainly, this aversion to seeming downbeat is behind the affection for Beavis and his pal Butt-Head, for Wayne and Garth, for Bill and Ted. In the eighties, we liked (perhaps shallowly) Tom Cruise in *Top Gun,* or Michael J. Fox in *Back to the Future,* or Charlie Sheen in the first two thirds of *Wall Street.* To like those figures was to assume a kind of responsibility. It was to make an admission. As Bret Ellis wrote in 1986, this was an admission that it would be a kick to be the best young fighter pilot in the air force, the savviest time traveler, the most cunning stock trader. The heroes in the present films have no such ambitions—and to like Beavis and Butt-Head is to hide what your ambitions are from anyone you might have confessed those ambitions to.

When journalists—like Leland, for example, like Howe and Strauss—write of us as "ironic," they are on to something. Irony develops in the absence of opportunity, *experienced in the presence of other people's opportunity.* When raw, likable appetite and ambition hold sway, other emotions are squeezed to the side for lack of time. But in the tantalizing absence of opportunity, we have irony. The tales we tell of ourselves follow a pattern—we become the comic, Don Quixote characters of our own stories. Look how much we wanted, and look what we got. The thwarted domestic tastes. How silly we were. There are few stories to tell of having gone out and effectively grabbed something. There is instead the detached story of how grabby we once were and how empty-handed we now are. We share in the humor of our plight with you.

But there is no question that had we come of age in an America of greater economic opportunity, or if opportunity returns to the country, we would show the values Americans have always shown. It puts the lie to all the things that have been written about us and spoken about us since the recession began. We are not "unprecedented"; we are not a strange new group with disturbing new attitudes. Does anyone really think that if we had money—and perhaps this is as regrettable as our old affection for Tom Cruise—we would be any different from what young American adults have always been?

Becoming an "adult" has always required some degree of sacrifice. We sally out young and full of beans and full of our *selves,* and come back a "certain type" of man or woman. That's the best we can hope for. Waiting for life to develop its predictable rhythm—the rhythm that allows us to run on confident automatic—which we as Americans both long for and deplore. Perhaps our disappointment lies in just this deferred personal *lessening.* This situation, in which we only and persistently become *more* ourselves, more our own unique and angular type of person, and not the soft-edged, well-fitting member of the community we secretly yearn to become. How delighted our parents once were to say of us, "A high school student." "A college boy." "A young woman." Now, there is no role for us but, "Alex again" or "David." The moment of transformation recedes into the future, as we forget what it would have meant, forget even that we were waiting for it.

Throughout our discussions with friends, peers, and strangers, we noticed an odd thing. The notion of "selling out" seemed to have vanished from the national vocabulary. Many people had to be reminded of what the term meant. "Selling out" had been a primary concern of the generations directly preceding ours—were they going to take the "easy" route and find a job in business, or were they going to try to do the harder thing, creating their own path and sticking to it? The culture has changed very much in the past twenty years. There has never been—as Leavitt and Johnson wrote in the mid-eighties about our generation—any question about whether selling out was the right choice or not. We had seen the importance of money from the very beginning. As Alexis de Tocqueville wrote in the 1830s, "The love of wealth is at the bottom of all that Americans do." We had seen this. Money is what buys freedom; money is what buys freedom from worrying about money.

None of the people we spoke with were fixated on being rich. They simply wanted to "get out from under." They wanted money to stop being the primary concern in their lives. They had the same values they had had in college and high school—and they were amused and unhappy about the portrait of themselves that had become accepted in the media. After all, their values had not changed. And in the thick of it, even as magazines continued to talk about "new values" among young people, the surveys conducted of high school students and college freshmen continued to report the same findings. Teenagers hoped to be married and professionally advanced within five years of graduation. "Being Well Off Financially" continued to be the major life goal of three quarters of college freshmen. "Developing a Meaningful Philosophy of Life" continued to idle around the 45 percent mark, despite the desire of older sociologists to shift this goal into a higher gear.

We got the worst of both worlds. If you strike out on your own, and flounder, at least you have the dignity of having failed at something noble. But when you start by "selling out," by simply trying to play the game as it has always been played, and fail, you have nothing to fall back on at all. Instead, the sadness of having been perfectly willing to "sell out"—eager to do so—and then finding no ready market for the goods. For the only product that really matters, your self, with your past experiences and the future skills you might bring to a company, to the country. People our age are in the position of disappointed pragmatists, of people who had decided they would give everything to getting ahead, and finding that goal very difficult to achieve. It leaves us with nothing at all—except irony, we suppose. The generation's life experience—and this is a more interesting story than the one *Time* gave us in 1990—is a historic *example* of irony.

We remain the people we were in college. The shift in reporting in the 1990s attempted to create a new character for our generation, a character that would be less disappointed by the country we would inherit as we stepped into adulthood. Perhaps these articles were trying to perform an unconscious kindness. After all, if we had *never* cared about adulthood and careers and marriage, it would be less painful for us if we could not achieve them. It would be less painful for the country of our parents, if they could believe that we had never been interested in such things. But we remain what we always were, regardless of fashions in reporting. Young people who want to grow up. Young people who want to achieve independence. Young people who want to *achieve*—who want to be tested and tried, praised and criticized, *incorporated*—who want to be adult Americans in the same way that generations of Americans have become adult.

Just how the country changed, and why the economy contracted so as not to offer us the chance at the adulthood we had wanted all along, is what we will talk about in our next chapter.

## ii.
# the bottom of all
# that americans do

"I think no one expects to stay at the same job for life. It's not like Japan where you bond with your company and you spend your entire working life with that company. I don't think people can rely on their company keeping them anymore, as they did in the seventies and eighties where you would, for example, stay with IBM forever. Now IBM is letting people go left and right and I think people now jump from job to job for money—and look out for themselves because they know they have to, and because you know your company isn't looking out for you anymore. I would have preferred the old system, of course. Everyone would. There's security—a job that you can count on having unless you choose to go someplace else. I don't think anyone's looking, in their early thirties, to have to go looking around for work."

—David Hoffberg, New York, New York, twenty-six

i.

# "golden opportunities"

—Fortune, *May 1985*

Mark Ferri graduated from the University of Michigan in 1987. Although interested in and adept at computers, he majored in art history, graduated with a fairly high average, and found himself . . . where? His father is a physician; his mother works in public relations. He sent résumés to ad agencies in New York and Detroit—and quickly found he was still nowhere. He had paid his school expenses by working part-time in a special effects house near Ann Arbor—he went back to this job, on a full-time basis, six months after graduation. It paid the same wages it had paid before graduation. His parents gave him the down money for a car and kept him on their health insurance plan. After a year at the special effects company—building models for supermarket ads in which high prices were vigorously exploded and affordable produce danced into the shopper's cart—he realized he would not be able to find a better job in either Detroit or New York without an advanced degree. Nor did he want to continue taking the small sums he regularly accepted from his understanding father, from his sympathetic mom. He enrolled in business school, for an MBA. He suffered through accounting and tax law. He re-sampled the pleasures, the low-level humiliations, the re-adolescence, of student life. In his last year at school, he attended the various on-campus interviews with Salomon Brothers, and Merrill Lynch, and G.E. He designed special résumés on his Macintosh, and did the sort of snap research in corporate practices that is presumed to increase one's odds and appeal as a candidate. But despite the letters he sent to firms of all kinds, in all states, he could not find a job. The representative from Salomon Brothers explained, during the second round of interviews, that she had been to nine other business schools, and at each there had been a group of fifty to a hundred graduates applying for spots. Mark raised his hand and asked, "How many positions are you offering at Salomon?" The representative answered, "One." Mark boarded a few months at his parent's home after graduation, went on interviews. Finally, in December, he moved back to Ann Arbor to resume his old job at the special effects company—the one job he had been offered during the four years since graduation. His increased familiarity with the Macintosh helped with some projects the company worked on—but at no increase of salary to him, as the entire ad industry was going through a long period of downsizing. He continued to accept small sums from his understanding father and sympathetic mom. Now, however, he was over twenty-six, and had to find his own health insurance plan.

Sonja Trojica grew up in Delaware, attended college in the Northeast, at a private university. This was done at her own expense—through loans for whose repayment she would become responsible six months after graduation. "Basically when it was time to go to college the money wasn't there. I wasn't surprised. I kind of knew it." Although she could have gone to her state university at "one tenth" the cost, "I chose my college to have the experience of being at a school with a better name. I thought it would affect my life by making me a different candidate, making me sort of looked at in a different way. I could have been a graduate of U. Delaware, but I was afraid I wouldn't get as good a job. I thought it would, sort of, lead me into higher positions. Make me more *appealing* to whomever. I'm now twelve thousand dollars in debt. I ponied up money through summer jobs. My folks probably put up two thousand a year." Sonja majored in French, hoping to teach after graduation, in her home state (with any luck) or in the Northeast. She found a job at a small private school in Wheeling, West Virginia— not a permanent post, but a one-year appointment with the possibility of a second one-year appointment upon completion. She had been dating the same man since college—they didn't intend to marry until both were more settled in their careers. At the end of the second year, the school told her there was no money on budget for a third year. She enrolled in the graduate program in English at the University of Delaware—this time, considerations of *appeal* were secondary, as the loans from her undergraduate education were difficult enough to manage. She graduated, and was able to find work in Lyons, France, teaching English. She and her boyfriend— who graduated from law school in 1991—moved there for two years, living on her teaching salary, until both became homesick. They moved back to America. They have been looking for work in their fields—Sonja as a teacher, her boyfriend as a lawyer—for six months. Now, both of them are homesick for *France*.

"I had my own little office, you know, my own place, my own job. Some mornings, I'd put on French music and have coffee and make believe. There was more opportunity there, in a sense." She and her boyfriend have married, and live together in his parent's home. "I'd simply say it's really hard getting a job right now. People aren't leaving their positions, and there are no new positions opening. Even for me to get accepted into graduate school was a really big deal. Because at that point, because jobs weren't around, people were deciding to go to graduate school. 'Oh let's go to graduate school.' There was this huge influx of prospective graduate students, and the competition was much harder, you know, because people who would not normally do it were going back."

At first, she and her husband had looked forward to the adventure of finding work. No longer. "To be honest, when we were facing this in France—because we knew neither one of us had a job—I actually was looking forward to the challenge. I was. 'Wow, we have all this open space in front of us. We have this opportunity to really go anywhere we want and do anything we want, and we can take our time.' Find jobs, the right jobs, the right place to be in our lives. Now that we're in the situation? I'm not as excited about it, only because I realize how difficult it is just getting started. I mean, the jump-starting. It's not happening, you know? I never thought it would last more than six months. I mean, this is unbelievable."

Ideally, of course, it wasn't supposed to be this way. The surprised young people who supplied quotations for news stories and television reports would all tell the same basic story. They had done what they were supposed to, and they weren't quite where they were supposed to be. "We were told since we were kids that if we worked hard, we would be success-ful. I worked hard, I had a high grade-point average, and I am one hundred percent overqualified for my job," a young woman, now a salesclerk, told *Business Week*. They had kept up their end of the bargain. Their papers were in order. And they were still working at the same jobs they had held, as stop-gap measures, *while* they were in college. As one kid told Barbara Walters, "They told us if you did A and B and C and D we could have it. But it's turned out not to be so sim-ple." There is the sense of a certain soft promise going un-kept, a personal pledge that has not been fulfilled.

More interesting, with a harder edge, it wasn't supposed to be this way *numerically* either. Demographically. During the eighties, when journalists were worrying about young people being too mature and calculating in their self-ad-vancement, demographers were telling them to relax. Time was in the process of curing all ills. Time was going to do our job search for us.

Many people our age are irritated by the term "baby bust," which has the sound of a kind of afterthought, a sad epilogue, to the baby boom. First the boom (great), then the bust (bad). In fact, the term has no comparison value what-soever. It has to do with birth rates. The boom started in the years after World War II—husbands were home from the army, finding great jobs, families were having three and four kids. The sixties put a stop to this—families went back to having one or two kids. It was supposed to be lucky for us, this membership in a baby bust. Economically lucky. It meant we would make more money. There would be less competition for jobs, we would have our pick of houses and rental units. Because there wouldn't be as many young adults to fill entry-level posts, employers would *have* to meet even our most outrageous demands (please don't assign projects on Thursday night, because that's when *Seinfeld* and *The Simpsons* are on). We were going to acquire things like careers and families and advancement rather casually, with the outward grasp of our fingertips. We were going to hit adulthood at a glide.

Richard Easterlin, an economist at USC, was the most vocal proponent of this theory. His 1980 book was called *Birth and Fortune*. Because our generation was so small, Easterlin said, "young men and women will encounter better job prospects. They will marry earlier, and will have more children." This prediction ran its victory lap through the presses. Wrote *Business Week* in the same era, "As for the baby bust generation, it will enjoy better entry-level jobs, higher relative incomes, and faster promotions because of sparser numbers. Indeed, new-found affluence will spur a rise in fertility and a return to the goal of large families." Not only were we not a sad afterthought, we were slated to become the parents of a *second* baby boom.

In the mid-eighties, magazines were writing of the coming "golden opportunities" it would be our tough task to differentiate among. In *Fortune*. In *Newsweek*. *Time* summarized this with typical breeziness in 1985: "The skimpier the generation, the more room at the table. Members of the baby bust will not face the teeming competition their parents did. They will struggle less and earn more. Rather like their grandparents. Sound familiar? They could just produce another baby boom and start the cycle over again." And there you have it. Not competition even for MAs in English, as Sonja described. Not hundreds of MBAs baying for a single Salomon Brothers position, as Mark related. Struggling less and earning more. Sounds like an unbeatable deal, doesn't it? The prediction continued to be made until the end of the decade—*Time* saw "higher salaries and more responsibility" on the wing in 1987—and the moment of truth was supposed to come in the early nineties, when a large segment of our generation reached its middle twenties.

Well, it's the middle nineties as we write this, and how did it turn out? With the age for first marriages at its highest level ever. With the size of families dropping to its smallest level. With almost one third of us unemployed. With the average incomes for those of us who were employed down 15 percent from what they had been in 1980, below those of the twentysomething baby boomers, and 35 percent lower than they would have been in the fifties, when our parents came out of college.

"More responsibility"—not a bad trade-off, if your salary is going to be low. You can hate the pay and love the work. This was the demographic hand that was supposed to have been invisibly working in our favor all along. How did it turn out? The demographic hand was making the noise of one hand clapping, as far as job opportunities were concerned. During the sixties, 36 percent of all newly created jobs were classified by the Department of Labor as professional or managerial (which also meant they were high paying). During the seventies, the percentage was even higher—44 percent. But by the mid-eighties—when people our age began coming out of college, to take advantage of their golden opportunities—only 28 percent of newly created jobs could be described as professional or managerial. Since the late eighties, the nation's number one job creator has been Wal-Mart. The number two job creator has been UPS. It turns out you can hate the pay *and* hate the work. During the 1960s and '70s, only one college graduate in ten drifted into a job that did not require a college degree—into the sad status the Bureau of Labor Statistics describes as "underemployed." By the 1980s, that number had increased to two college graduates in ten. By the early 1990s, three in ten of us left college to immediately find ourselves "underemployed."

So a young adult member of the baby bust was three times more likely than a young adult member of the baby boom to be poorly paid and in a low-skill job; we were three times more likely to have *lower* salaries and *less* responsibility. The reverse of a situation in which we would outperform the baby boom; the reverse of "golden opportunities." When we contacted Professor Easterlin in the fall of 1993, to ask him what had happened, he asked our birth years. Then he laughed and said, "You were born ten years too soon."

ii.

"there's no getting away
from the fact that
graduates themselves
are doing something wrong.
they simply don't know
how to get hired."
—Forbes, *December 1984*

Everyone knows *somebody* who is able to make money during hard times—whose drive is so pure that it doesn't much matter what financial music their era is playing. But very few of us are those indestructible economic Frankensteins. The hard numerical fact was that if you were in your early to late twenties in the 1990s, you weren't going to be making much money, because you weren't going to find a terrific job. If you're twentysomething, it's important to keep a handle on that. We're an optimistic country, but the flip side of optimism is blame: Everyone can get ahead if they really want to, so if you're not getting ahead, you must not want to. If you're the parent of a twentysomething, and your kid is asking for cash, or isn't quite the sensation at family dinners she was in 1985 or 1975, it's important to keep your eye on the numbers. On this number, in particular: Between 1990 and 1993, three million of us graduated from American universities. In the same period, only 870,000 new American payroll jobs were created. (And this is not to mention the one million of us who lost jobs from May 1990 to May 1991.) Numbers like those were going to mean a shake-out.

For the last twenty years, America has been a decreasingly terrific place for young people. It's been a kind of slow downward drag, and it was interrupted for only three or four years, in the mid-1980s. This was the period when the government borrowed trillions from the Japanese and from the Americans of Tomorrow (to borrow a Disneyland phrase) to fight a war against a bad mood. It was a war against the malaise of the seventies, a war against the notion that America was entering a period of slow downward drag. America won. We scared the Soviets into submission, with the sheer weight of our borrowing power. But now that war is over. We're back in the position we were in before the 1980s, where we're all afraid that America is on a kind of slow downward drag.

People have talked about the Britainization of America—that we might be following in England's sorry footsteps as a once-dominant power that let its image go to its head and then frittered everything away. You could read about this in long cover stories in *The Atlantic,* in Kevin Phillips's book *The Politics of Rich and Poor.* It is just one of those ideas that's been drifting around.

So let's look at England—England, which seems to have gotten there ahead of us, at least with regard to being a not-great country for the young. The Martin Amis excerpt in our introduction comes from his novel *Success*. By 1978, young people in England were scared silly by the leaden opportunities their country was offering up. According to *Success*, 1978 London is a place where "the money lasted my parents' time. It won't last mine." It's a city where young characters read "quite shrewd articles on the economic collapse," where "disgruntlement hangs in the air like a migraine," where people dread layoffs because "there are no new jobs and nobody wants to go looking for them." Where, as one young character describes his work, "My job is, and always has been (to put it mildly), *fucking awful*. It is a daily round of boredom and humiliation, with no prospects and no rewards."

Amis is a hyperbolist, and one could argue that the America of our parents, of older people, hasn't become England yet, regardless of Kevin Phillips's or Pete Peterson's fears. But the America of the young has—or feels like it—and you could probably slip the two Amis passages into the novel *Generation X* without anyone noticing they weren't reading Douglas Coupland. *Generation X,* by the way, was published in 1991.

Every year, the career placement service at Northwestern University issues the Lindquist-Endicott Survey—which is where national newspapers get their forecasts for postgraduate jobs. In the spring, Victor Lindquist asks recruiters how many graduates they are likely to hire; in the fall, in a follow-up report, he asks how many got hired. Here's how postgraduate opportunity has shaped up since 1980, at least according to the Lindquist survey.

1980: Okay.

1981: Soft (down 25 percent from 1980).

1982: Lousy. (Recession pops up. Engineers, however, have easy time, and will continue to do so until the end of the decade.)

1983: Awful. (11 percent worse than 1982. *The New York Times* says, "depression levels.")

1984: Soft. ("Job openings at individual firms will be down from their prerecession levels" [*U.S. News & World Report*]—that is, from the soft 1981 numbers.)

1985: Okay. (15 percent higher than 1984; overture to Reagan boom. Salaries, however, remain unimproved.)

1986: Good. ("The revolution of rising expectation continues for the class of 1986," jokes A. Whitney Brown on *Saturday Night Live*'s "Weekend Update.")

1987: Good.

1988: Good. ("The class of '88 is in luck," [*U.S. News*], although salaries—those dawdlers!—still lag behind inflation.)

1989: Soft (10 percent lower than 1988).

1990: Awful. (GM and IBM cancel on-campus interviews, and establish hiring freeze. Recession officially begins in July. Lindquist euphemizes, "It's going to be quite competitive for the new grads.")

1991: Lousy again. (15 percent drop from bad 1990 numbers. Engineers beginning to face nonhiring. Says one career counselor, "We around here are saying it's the worst year since 1945.")

1992: Lousier. (Lindquist, who has prepared survey every year since 1958, declares, "I've never seen a tougher market for college grads." Job offers this year down 45 percent from 1989's already-soft numbers. Bureau of Labor Statistics predicts that present conditions—low responsibility, low pay—likely to continue for young people into year 2005.)

1993: Worse again. (College Placement Council reports 25 percent drop in hiring over 1992. Anthropologist Karen Newman tells *The New York Times*, "On virtually all counts it was better to have reached adulthood by the early 1950s than at almost any time afterward." She continues, "The older generation doesn't quite get why hard work doesn't do for their children what it did for them." Nor does Newman see any transforming and wonderful change arrowing in from the horizon: "I'm without much confidence that this is temporary.")

Not very encouraging, is it? Any discussion of the behavior of our generation has to start here—where else could it start? We are delaying marriage and balking at starting careers? People won't marry if they can't bring at least the presumption of self-sufficiency to the altar; they can't begin their careers if they aren't being hired. The numbers explain why Amis's sixteen-year-old description of London feels so oddly modern. In fourteen college graduations since 1980, there have been only four certifiably "good" years; everything else has been either soft or lousy. Everything else has been bad. By 1992, according to the Lindquist-Endicott Survey, companies were hiring a full 20 percent fewer college graduates than they had been a decade earlier, even though graduating classes were now one third larger. Most painful, in researching these years, have been the many moments—in interviews, in articles—when people our age would wonder if they had done something wrong, if their poor showing, their poor salary, was the aggregate of a number of bad choices they had made. It's natural—the way you will feel obscenely singled out if a stranger smacks you with a snowball from a passing car. We wanted to take these people aside and whisper, "Look, look. We know you tried hard; you probably could have tried harder, maybe, if you really wanted to, but it wouldn't have mattered much. Look at these numbers. You didn't really have a chance. You were born twenty years too late, or ten years too early. Look. We got hit by the same snowball."

On the telephone, Victor Lindquist is a charming, concerned, and warm-voiced presence. He has developed the media person's knack of speaking in full, grammatically correct sentences. He is eager to chat, about what he calls the "myths" in the culture—that young people have changed their basic goals, that they are no longer interested in financial stability, that their work ethic has vanished. "Not true. Not true at all." He worries about the emotional impact of prolonged unemployment. "There's all the psychic income that one draws. It's almost a necessity towards being a complete individual. To have a fulfilling job *makes* you a fulfilled individual. Not to have one? Well . . ."

Was it easier to get a job in other decades? "The workplace for young people has changed enormously in three and a half decades. In the fifties, sixties, and even the seventies there was a demand for college graduates. When I came out of graduate school in 1958, there was some concern on the part of students at that time. But while one might be concerned about *having* a job, there was far more confidence on the part of graduates that they would go out and be able to find *something* that would allow them to put their foot on the first rung of the career ladder." How does Lindquist, who has been counseling college graduates since the late fifties, sum up employment in the nineties? "This is the worst I've seen in thirty years." Says Lindquist, "The realities are very different in 1993 than they were in 1983. When you look back over the last ten years, the changes have been almost cataclysmic."

With this information available, you would think journalists would be chary of reporting anything but the numbers. Instead, they have concentrated on the personal—congratulating graduates for "determination and competitiveness" in years when there were jobs to be had, blaming them for laziness when jobs were gone. In 1984, after two not-great years, *Forbes* sourly observed, "There's no getting away from the fact that graduates themselves are doing something wrong. They simply don't know how to get hired." In 1986, after two years of the Reagan boom, *Forbes* was writing articles about supergraduates that now have the lost, comic tone of Horatio Alger stories written for a different planet. "After pulling an all-nighter to proofread, photocopy, and bind the brochure, [twenty-four-year-old Steve] Finnegan hopped a flight to Chicago in the same jeans and sweatshirt he'd been wearing all week. When he showed up at Beatrice unshaven, in running shoes, looking like an unkempt messenger boy, only to be introduced as a member of Salomon's merger and acquisition group, the Beatrice people had a hearty laugh. Finnegan has the last laugh, however. He was just accepted to Harvard Business School." It was as if journalists believed graduates who came out of school in strong years were more talented, better adapted, than graduates who emerged in weak ones. The obvious fact—that when there were jobs to be had students would find them—seems to have been elusive.

What's bad—by our lights—about any discussion of our character that ignores the economy is that it leads people to believe that values ricochet back and forth, when it's really only the economy that does so. Parents who read the *Forbes* articles in the late eighties would wonder why their own children weren't jetting in charmingly ratty garments to Chicago; parents who read articles in the nineties would wonder what had happened to the ambitions of their kids. If you read all the demographic articles saying how easy things were going to get for us, you were confused by where you actually ended up. In the nineties, with the economy going rotten again, blame made its comeback. Once again students no longer "knew how to get hired." *Time* explained, in 1990, "While recruiters are trying to woo young workers, a generation is out planning its escape from the 9-to-5 routine." What a horrible way to put it—and what a wrongful thing to make parents, employers, and people our age think. Obviously, there weren't as many graduates with steady employment in 1990 as there'd been the preceding years. But it was the recruiters who had "escaped," not the generation—and looking at the numbers shows just when they left, and just how long they have been away.

### iii.
### "the economics of joy"
—Fortune, *December 1982*

What made the economy go south in the late eighties? Two things: The national debt was causing the country tremendous trouble, and the *nature* of employment had dramatically changed.

Looking ahead—without foreseeing the expansion of debt and the change in employment—economists like Easterlin had in 1980 seen lots of money coming our way. Numbers were on our side. Certainly, the debt changed that.

We all know it's wrong to look to the government to solve our economic problems. It's dirty pool, like asking a teacher to suggest answers during an exam: It's better, and in the long run healthier, to solve problems on your own. On the other hand, during recession, our government has traditionally had one option available to improve conditions. It can increase spending. This creates jobs—for public workers and the industries that love them, as the self-help books might put it. The economy starts rolling again, and everybody's happy. The recession of 1990 was triggered by a number of factors that weren't our fault—by things that happened while we were out of the room, attending to our business of getting older and going to college. The Leveraged Buyout decade, the stock market crash, the deficit itself: the downsizing of corporations that once hired young people was initiated to remedy these problems. We didn't share in the fun, but we ended up sharing in the aftermath—and the one positive response the government had to such conditions had been X-ed out of the picture. Coming into the 1990 recession, the government couldn't spend its way out—it was too busy paying off deficits from the *last* recession. We didn't get a chance to join in the frenzy that caused the problem, and government had frittered away its solution. Bad luck. As Murray Weidenbaum, Reagan's first chairman of the Council of Economic Advisers, put it, "It's hard to explain. The farther away in time one gets, the harder it is to explain. Something from 1981 is determining the present."

What brought on the debt? Coming out of the seventies, the economy was not so great. In many ways, you could argue, we've been cycled back into the unsolved problems of the seventies, with this added burden of borrowing. The Japanese had done their thing with the auto market; OPEC had raised oil prices twice, driving up the cost of most other items as well. America was in for a period of slow growth before we'd be in the clear. By the mid-eighties, things would have straightened out—which would have been perfectly fine by us. Late seventies' economists and business leaders merely hoped that Carter—president then, and about to face re-election—would not knuckle under to political imperatives and increase deficit spending. Deficit spending would ease problems in the short term, leave problems in the long. Carter chose not to spend through a deficit.

There were other factors: The sociologist James Coleman, who had tracked the baby boomers since the early seventies, saw the problem coming in 1978. The generation was so big—one third of all citizens—that it would have an immediate impact on national policies. "One thing we can expect is a serious conflict between the interests of the affluent, whose interests lie in the direction of no economic growth, and the interests of those who can only make it if there is economic growth." Christopher Lasch, a historian and author of *The Culture of Narcissism,* had been following value changes over the decade. His book's main argument was that the country had become radically self-involved. That the traditional interest Americans took in the fate of others had disappeared—that the country had lost interest not only in present-day others but in *future* others. Wrote Lasch in 1979, "To live for the moment is the prevailing passion—to live for yourself, not for posterity. A society that fears it has no future is not likely to give much thought to the needs of the next generation. [Our] society has lost interest in the future."

In this atmosphere, it is not surprising that when Ronald Reagan was elected and began to spend against future earnings, no one really protested. (We can tell they didn't protest, because here we are with these huge deficits.) What's lovable about this information is this: People our age have been tarred—unreasonably, we'd say—for not wanting to work, for wanting to get something for nothing. ("If there is a bumper sticker that fits today's twentysomethings," opined the *Chicago Tribune* in 1992, "it would read 'Earn the maximum for the minimum.'") This attitude is sensibly called childish. Yet even if it were true, it would have the advantage of affecting only us: We'd have lousy jobs. But the behavior of the government during the eighties—wanting the maximum of voter affection with the minimum of tax resentment—represented childishness on a global scale. And it *did* affect others.

The economist David Stockman has been called "the driving force behind Ronald Reagan's economic policy." He was director of the Office of Management and Budget during Reagan's first term. In July of 1993, he agreed to a long mea culpa interview with Sidney Blumenthal in *The New Yorker*. What Stockman said about the Reagan debts was spooky—and spookier still was that the article received little attention. According to Stockman, the deficits have affected almost all government policy since they were created. Further, people in government knew how large they were going to be and didn't *care*. Said Stockman, "The job of every president since Reagan—a sunshine boy who didn't want to acknowledge that the deficit was his problem—is to distribute and administer pain. Clinton is mired neck deep. . . . It was really an unnecessary chapter."

Reagan ran on tax cuts—the idea being that if you cut taxes, more money would end up being spent in the economy, and the government would end up receiving more in taxes anyway. ("Earn the maximum for the minimum.")

Stockman told Blumenthal, "There hadn't been large-scale fiscal politics practiced earlier. The budget, on its own momentum, was always close to balanced. It would cycle up a bit. If you didn't do anything, there was no harm done. Basically, the underlying fundamentals were sound. It fell apart in 1981 with the tax-cut bill, and you entered the opposite world."

When Stockman checked the figures of the tax cut, he recognized that they might not add up—that they might leave the country with unmanageably large deficits. In the summer of 1981, he argued for a public admission to this effect. James Baker, George Bush's principal aide, asked, "You mean, it really is voodoo economics, after all?" Yet Baker and others in the administration argued for going ahead with the tax cuts anyway: Long-term economic consequences were subordinated to immediate political popularity. The Democrats were no more honest than the Republicans—sensing the political mood of the country, they joined right in. Although Stockman told *The Atlantic* in 1981 that, "None of us really understand what's going on with all these numbers," the cuts proved immensely popular. American voters were paying lower taxes and getting the same level of government service. In 1988, Baker encouraged George Bush to make his "no new taxes" pledge—although most people in government agreed that taxes would have to be raised by the new president. When Dan Rostenkowski complained, "What are you doing?" Baker replied, "We're going to elect a president of the United States. We'll talk about *that* after he's elected." As Sidney Blumenthal put it, "The lesson of Reagan seemed to be that fiscal policy could be finessed indefinitely." As Stockman put it, "It was a tremendous mistake."

Between them, Reagan and Bush cobbled together three

trillion dollars of new debt in twelve years. All told, the thirty-nine presidents *before* Bush and Reagan had managed to accumulate only eight hundred billion dollars of debt. It's a comparatively sorry showing. And it wasn't as if no one was thinking about who was going to end up paying for it. That's the ironic part. Most people *knew*. The concern that it would be young people, at the end of the century, who would end up signing the checks was ever-present. But it was voodoo concern. To state the problem meant you could go ahead and enact dangerous policies with a clear conscience—you had at least shown you were fully aware of the risks. Reading the debate of that time is like hearing the three little pigs discuss how much really better and safer it would be to build a brick house, while continuing to live in the straw one.

Herbert Stein, who chaired the Council of Economic Advisers under Nixon, wrote a long warning on the debt in 1982. Americans, he said, had wanted an end to inflation, a rise in incomes, and a restoration of America to military prominence. The president promised to do these things while at the same time cutting their taxes. "This was the economics of joy," wrote Stein. "The economics of joy is simple, painless, and salable. It is also unrealistic."

By late 1981, "reality flooded in" and "deficits suddenly looked large and endless." By December of 1982, Stein could write, "Great concern is being expressed in the country about deficits. But our alarm about the deficits does not lead to decisive action; the size of deficits rises, and the threshold at which we become alarmed also rises." Why was there no decisive action? Stein was frank. "The reason we won't do much is that we don't really care much. Reducing the deficit requires giving up something, and no one is willing to eliminate much except the other fellow's program or the other fellow's tax cut. Why don't we care more? The reason is that the real consequences of deficits come years in the future. The total deficits of the 1980s will have a large effect on the size of the capital stock in the 1990s, and therefore on the income of people living in the 1990s. To be concerned about the income of the nation as a whole in the next generation requires a lot of understanding, foresight, and civic spirit. So we are probably destined to live with large deficits for a long time."

In 1984, W. R. Grace ran a scare ad about the debt—a baby girl is born, two bureaucrats show up and inform her she now owes the government fifty thousand dollars. The baby initials their contract with an inky footprint. Peter Grace (who knows with what mix of altruism and self-advancement) hoped to make Americans appreciate the consequences of spending against the future. After a few months, NBC pulled the ad, saying it was "too controversial." A year later, Grace hired director Ridley Scott to produce a second deficit ad. This was set in a courtroom of the future, with a group of impoverished kids questioning an older man as to why, in the eighties, government had let deficits go ruinously out of control. "Will you ever forgive us?" the older man asks. This ad was rejected by all three networks, as being too controversial.

In 1985, the governor of Ohio wrote an editorial called "Borrowing from Our Children," warning who the deficits were going to affect. "The generation currently running America is made up of prodigal parents," Governor Lamm wrote. "We have enriched ourselves at the expense of our children. We have mortgaged their future to pay for our excesses. Each generation encounters its own historical challenge, the outcome of which leaves a legacy of opportunities and challenges for the next generation. We inherited abundance and opportunity; we are leaving mortgages and encumbrances. Through our reluctance to make tough decisions today, we are bequeathing to our children even higher taxes than we have had to pay. Every year of political inaction means our children will have less money to spend on food, clothes, cars, housing, their children's education, and other elements of a decent standard of living. We are borrowing from our children and our grandchildren." The governor predicted that a major political issue of the future would be "intergenerational equity, when we are called by our children to account for our excesses." Deficits throughout these years continued to increase.

In 1989, in *The Atlantic,* the political observer Jonathan Rauch could write that continuing deficits showed that "Americans had changed their attitudes about the morality of borrowing against the future." Two years earlier, in the same magazine, former secretary of commerce Pete Peterson had made the same observation. He wrote a tremendously long cover story about the debt called "The Morning After." In it, he argued passionately that the eighties had manifested "the worst, future-averting choices America has ever made, the full implications of which will not be known for years." According to Peterson, the massive borrowing of the eighties, coming on the heels of the disappointing seventies, had created a make-believe sixties: "a decade of 'feeling good' and 'having it all'—without the bother of producing a real one." According to Peterson, this nice decade was funded at the expense of the next generation. As he wrote, "If before the 1980s, [the] manner in which American public policy treats our future was one of neglect, today it borders on open contempt."

Peterson warned that, as of 1987, America faced a future of economic choices "far less pleasant than any set of choices we have confronted in living memory." By Peterson's calculations, what the eighties gave the country—increased consumption and a higher standard of living—the nineties were probably going to take away. At our expense.

Peterson became likably passionate on the topic. "Our children represent the furthest living reach of posterity, the only compelling reason that we have to be serious about investing in the future. And we are failing them. Soon we must stop, [or] else forever relegate those children to slower growth in their standard of living." Wrote Peterson, "If each generation insists on its 'right' to consume all its own product and part of the next generation's as well, then we can count on a meager and strife-torn future." As Peterson warned, "The 1980s and 1990s may be remembered, with bitterness, as a turning point in America's fortunes—a period of transition when we took the British route to second-class economic status." Which brings us back to Martin Amis, and why seventies London feels so much like nineties New York, like nineties Los Angeles, Washington, and Chicago.

By 1993, you could generalize about the effects of the debt. They were bad. The eight-hundred-billion-dollar debt of 1980 had represented about 30 percent of the Gross Domestic Product. This means that if, with a magnificent gesture, we had decided to use the value of all goods and services produced in the country in 1980 to pay off the red ink of more than two hundred years of American government, we would still have had 70 percent left over. By 1993, the proportions were exactly reversed. The total debt was 4.4 trillion dollars. If President Clinton had decided to make that berserk and magnificent gesture, it would have absorbed 70 percent of our Gross Domestic Product, leaving behind only 30 percent. There's your shift in the country. Interest payments were absorbing one fourth of every tax dollar. You couldn't have new spending; indeed, a good part of deficit spending went to paying the note on the old deficits. And most economists now agreed that the debt "prolonged the recession" by slowing growth—William Branson, a professor of economics at Princeton, calculated that the 1992 growth rate would have been 50 percent higher without the "drag" from the debt.

With slow growth, there were fewer jobs, which paid less. With higher taxes, and no stimulative spending, government could at worst be a drain and at best not a boon. It was the exact turn of events observers had foreseen in the mid-eighties. The advantage of being in a small generation—having all those goodies stockpiled up ahead of you—was erased by the debt. The opportunities we might have had were instead used as fuel during a period when we were off pursuing our educations. When we came out, the climate had radically altered from what we and those late-seventies economists had expected it to be.

iv.
## "english can be a marketable skill."
—Money, *March 1992*

Reviewing this material makes it easier to understand why young people like Sonja and Mark have had such a hard time finding jobs—it is easier for us to understand it than it is for them. Through the late eighties and early nineties, college-educated young people would report, "My friends don't know what to do. They simply cannot find work." Some would blame the generations before ours, using a standard "party" analogy: Others had thrown a party, and we were being asked to clean up after it, to foot the bill. The analogy became so overused that it was easy to disregard—it became poor English. But it was accurate; you could disregard it aesthetically, but not economically.

How much did the climate change? In 1984, a writer in *Forbes* warned young people to stay away from low-wage jobs. "The most common opening is as a salesclerk, and what needs to be pointed out about the position is that it is nearly always a dead-end job. Youngsters full of enthusiasm don't believe this. They think their sales ability will see them through and speed their rise. The argument that these jobs are 'valuable work experience' needs to be refuted bluntly. Few employers place much value on this type of labor. It can be done by almost anyone." By 1993, journalists were giving entirely opposite advice: We should take any job we were lucky enough to find. "There is no golden ticket for college graduates, so any workplace background is better than none, and ingenuity impresses employers" (the *Chicago Tribune*). "Go ahead, take a short-term job. Accept an internship. Work for free on a trial basis to prove your worth" (the Cleveland *Plain Dealer*).

Sonja Trojica had gone in 1991 to Lyons to find work, and is considering returning. "If I went back to France right now, I could get a job. I am a very sellable commodity there." What commodity does Sonja have in France that she doesn't have in the United States? "I'm a native English speaker. It's weird in a sense. I went to one of the top colleges in the country, and yet I'm a better quantity overseas. Because everyone's interested in learning English. English is the language of the European Community, and it is the language of the world. All businesses, multinational, whatever, require that their employees speak English. I sold my English."

Sonja thought her experience was an anomaly. But in fact it was good solid behavior, a clever subscription to the dominant job-market advice. In March of 1992, when *Money* magazine published an article called "Three Tips to Help New Grads Land a First Job," the suggestions showed just how much the economy had changed in thirteen years. The tips were: "1) Volunteer at a nonprofit. 2) Get a foot in the door you want. You may be able to invent your own internship. 3) Go overseas. English can be a marketable skill." It didn't occur to anyone that for the first two you would have to have an independent source of income (how else could you survive without pay?). Nor did it seem to surprise anyone that for the third—if you had unwisely chosen not to be born rich—it was necessary to leave the country. The article was just a little glimmer in its magazine, like the Stockman remarks about the debt, and like the Stockman remarks it just slipped right by. But it packed its punch. It spoke eloquently and powerfully about what it meant, in the 1990s, to be young in America.

# iii.
# the disappearance of childhood

"That's exactly what I'm saying. I think like the stuff when people talk about that whole slacker culture: How about attributing it to having been an adult at age ten? And now I'm just—I'm tired. I want to play in the sandbox. I want to sit on the couch and toss bonbons into my mouth. Like retired people when they move down to Florida. Yeah. I swear, my apartment somtimes feels like a retirement community for people in their twenties who don't want to do anything. I don't know anybody who seems really to have caught up. Maybe we'll all get our second winds at age thirty-two. I hope I get my second wind tomorrow."

—Eileen Wallace, Chicago, Illinois, twenty-seven

i.

"ricky helps edward
to be an adult
and edward teaches his son
the pleasures of childhood."
—*NBC press release for* Silver Spoons, *1982*

Twentysomethings have the knack of showing up at the end of something. *Right* at the end, so that we know what it was supposed to have been like—but where is it? We dash after retreating images. As a generation, we seem to be constantly shouting *hey, wait!* as the airplane leaves the gate, as the bus pulls away in its riot of noise and dust. Hey, wait! There had been a period of pretty easy living in America for a long time, heightened by the wild borrowing of the eighties; twenty-eight-year-olds were making two hundred thousand a year—Christ, you just missed it. It was here a second ago. After about a century of repression, starting in the late sixties there was a twenty-year phase of real experimentation with sex, and then—whoops. Slip this thing on over the business end, pal, try to keep a lid on it, sister, or you're dead. (If you were gay, there'd been over two centuries of repression, and this was even worse.) Once upon a time you could go to college without spending a lot of cash, and have a pretty good time while you were there—but not so fast. Now you're going to be ten thousand dollars in debt when you graduate, so you'd better not spend sophomore year in a stupor.

The constant factor in our experience as a generation has been just this *lack* of constancy—we're perpetually hammering on the door of a bar fifteen minutes after the staff has already locked away the bottles and put up the glasses for the night. If you could generalize about the baby boomers—and who, secretly, doesn't want to do just that?—you would say they are a generation that always decides, just at the last moment, that they would prefer to knuckle under. Look at Dustin Hoffman at the end of *The Graduate*—he realizes that all in all he'd like to be a young-married, runs to church, and rescues Katherine Ross just in time. If *The Graduate* were about late bloomers, Dustin Hoffman would show up one hour too late to discover the wedding already concluded and a photographer putting away his film and only a few slivers of rice left in the grass, for anthropology's sake.

But let's not generalize too much. Let's start at the beginning, with our childhoods. We were born from the early sixties to the mid-seventies. Two decades later, when journalists were trying to account for our difficulty engaging with the economy, they would point to our upbringings. These had been too soft. As *Money* magazine explained, "They have failed to develop a sense of self-sufficiency because they have always been handed the best of everything. When they are finally asked to become their own masters, their fragile hothouse egos wilt." How much does this have to do with childhood in the 1970s?

We still had pretty standard toddlerhoods. But by the time we were kids—thinking midgets—the divorce boom was starting. The women-into-the-workforce movement was running at full throttle. A lot of this was economic—the American standard of living had more or less peaked in 1973, so it was now *necessary* for mothers to work. Once they were working, they had their own cash, and it was no longer necessary to stay in bad marriages the way their own mothers had. So family life changed a lot. For at least a century you'd had this ideal of one wage-earner, one child-raiser. The children were the beneficiaries of this arrangement, getting fat off the fruits of their parents' sacrifices. *No más.*

Of course, one constant in *American* life—as opposed to just the life cycle of our generation—has been this fear of slippage in the family. Like the dismay about the work ethic, America has been haunted by the sense, in every era, that family life is going to the dogs. Perhaps, like the work ethic, being a parent is one of the things we simply are not entirely comfortable doing. Worrying about the work ethic, or the family, is a way of confessing that if there were not very strict social prohibitions, we'd probably blow it off. We would all pull a pillow over our heads while the baby cried, or spend money not for the kid's new clothing but for our own.

You see it every few decades, this sense that it was *better,* easier, more *natural* to raise kids at some other time than it is today. Social commentators in the eighties and nineties would point back to the fifties and say, There, then, we had this problem under control. *That's* when we did our child rearing with certainty. (One book complained that between the fifties and the eighties family life had undergone a transformation "from *My Three Sons* to *My Two Dads*"—without realizing that this meant there had been no transformation, since the comic premise of *My Three Sons* had been that the children had, in Fred MacMurray as Dad and William Demarest as Uncle Charlie, two fathers.) Go back to the fifties, however, and you find that sociologists like David Reisman also felt family life was going to the dogs. The *forties*, the *thirties*—that was the golden era, apparently; those were the days when parents could go about child rearing with certainty. Christopher Lasch, in his witty *Narcissism* book, includes pages of this kind of nostalgia for the lost family, cropping up in—at all times—the 1930s, the 1910s, when you or I would feel that people probably *did* have the family problem under control. Mom and Dad probably really did keep the lid on things. In their long article in *The Atlantic*, Neil Howe and William Strauss included a letter written by a young person claiming that since he and his peers had grown up at a time when the family was under siege, when there was no family at all, they had been forced to raise themselves, and were much the worse for it. The letter was from 1911. (Strauss and Howe's book *13th Gen* was far less clever than the article, which was written for people their own age. The book was written for people our age, so it wasn't really written for anybody. It was written for a demographic category corresponding to our age. It was written for nobody.) In Lasch's book, people in the 1880s felt people in the *1850s* had had the lock on child rearing.

So you should take it with some cynicism when we say that in the seventies and eighties the family really *did* fall apart, and we really *did* raise ourselves. We can imagine a vantage point in the next century, when kids are raised by anthropomorphic chimpanzees or hospitable robots, from which what we say about how family life has gone to the dogs will seem ridiculous. But from *this* vantage point, in 1994, throughout the period those fears were being expressed—the 1910s, the 1930s, the 1950s—family life looks pretty unchanged. Divorce was rare. Working mothers probably rarer. (Between 1960 and 1980 the number of working mothers with children under five more than doubled—from 20 percent to 47 percent.) The shift came in the seventies—it was as if the culture had been preparing for the change all century, and then when it came, there had been no structure prepared to deal with it. Everyone was caught by surprise, by a shift they had fretted over for fifty years. We aren't blaming anyone in particular—this is meant as a no-fault discussion. We late bloomers were merely in the wrong place at the wrong time. We seem fated always to be the experimental group, never the control.

By the mid-seventies, sociologists were warning that the nuclear family, "the basic unit of society," was being "destabilized to an enormous degree." Said a professor from the University of Chicago, "We are becoming the first species in the history of the world which is unable to care for its young." The new "instability of marriage" meant that children were now very often going to be the product of broken homes. "But the concept of a complete household," Professor James Coleman said, "has been undermined so much that we now just call them single-parent households." Overall, Professor Coleman found child rearing was one of the great casualties of the modern age. He continued, "Of all the changes in society, I think this breakdown of the family is going to prove to be the most powerful, the most destructive and the most enduring." The Stanford economist Victor Fuchs, writing in 1983, argued the same points—the combination of working mothers and divorcing parents was altering the nature of the family in ways it had never been altered before.

The change was that with parents around for less of the day—if your parents were divorced, as half our parents were, and both those parents were working, they weren't going to be around in the afternoons—kids really *did* raise themselves. You can see the nostalgia the baby boomers have for their childhoods in shows like *The Wonder Years,* or in the foggy-edged "reminiscence" scenes in *thirtysomething.* Childhood is seen as a simple time with minimal but telling surprises. Your dad has a job, you visit, and he doesn't have the same respect at his office—wow!—that he demands at home. Your mother and father argue about money, panic when you overhear—whoops!—then take you aside and explain that adults love each other even when they fight. Anyway, you're becoming a man now, and soon you'll understand. The expression in little Fred Savage's eyes (with Daniel Stern's kooky narration highlighting the lessons) is that these slow exposures to the adult world are *strengthening* toward the time when Fred Savage will improbably elongate to become Daniel Stern, when Ken Olin will start his own ad agency.

With the combination of divorce and working mothers, you no longer had the slow exposure. You got total immersion. Our parents were revealed not as distant and mysterious bodies—planets you might get vivid and occasional glimpses of through a telescope—but as costrugglers in the world, who might even ask our advice. When you talk to people our age about their childhoods, they don't have nostalgia for their stint as children. ("I mostly wanted to grow up, get out, and make a life for myself that was more predictable," one woman wrote to us.) What they have is nostalgia for the *television programs* they watched. Who among us has not, at one time or another, wished to be one of the Partridges, one of the Bradys?

This was the third big change: television and movies. The first books about childhood in the eighties pointed to the fact. First, you had kids who were left alone a good deal of the time, kids who picked up the slack of caring for their younger brothers and sisters that their parents couldn't hold anymore. Second, you had kids from families that had dissolved. (The American divorce rate nearly tripled between 1960 and 1979, from nine per thousand couples per year to nearly twenty-three. By 1986, it was the highest in the Western world. In the full global competition, it finished fourth, edged aside by Liechtenstein, the Maldives, and Peru.) Third, you had kids getting their primary information about the world not through the experiences of their folks but through pictures on television.

And the pictures were of a radically different order than the pictures seen by the baby boom. The boomers, officially, were the first generation to be raised in the world of television. But television, in the fifties and sixties, was very different than it was in the seventies. In this earlier era, television still functioned as a kind of national propaganda arm. It was still allowed to portray only what the culture pretended to believe about itself—that all parents were stalwart, that most strangers were good. Eight hours a day spent in front of the TV in 1955 wouldn't leave you hearing anything, essentially, that a sixth-grade teacher wouldn't have been comfortable having you hear. The content of a sixth-grade classroom and a 1955 sitcom was quite similar: Behave properly. Work hard. Obey your parents. You'll be fine. By the seventies, TV was no longer a medium in which only good thoughts held sway—and by an unlucky quirk of history, that was exactly the time when parents were disappearing from their children's homes, so that TV would take an even greater hold of their world view. A program like the late fifties' *Donna Reed Show* demonstrated how family life was supposed to go. A program like the seventies' *One Day at a Time* (with its scary and exhausted title) showed more or less how things actually went.

This was the point Neil Postman made in his 1982 book

*The Disappearance of Childhood.* (An earlier book, *The Hurried Child: Growing Up Too Fast, Too Soon,* had been written by the psychiatrist David Elkind in 1981.) Where was childhood disappearing to? Reruns from the fifties. What was it turning into? Adulthood. The *state* of childhood was disappearing. Children remained, however—there goes the bus!—and were instead becoming little adults. Television was exposing children to far too many things, erasing the old dividing line between what adults knew and what children knew. There was once a notion that there were, as Postman put it, "certain facets of adult life—its mysteries, its contradictions, its violences, its tragedies—that are not considered suitable for a child to see." TV gave this the heave-ho. Postman called television "the first curriculum." He called it that because the set was where children did much of their most powerful learning about what society was like. An average child would spend only 13,000 hours in school before age eighteen. The same kid would spend 23,000 hours watching television. Elizabeth Crow, then editor of *Parents* magazine, made the same point. In a 1982 *Washington Post* article called "Where Have All the Children Gone?" Crow said, "Parents proudly urge children to earn their own keep and to be their pals, not their charges, and the notion that children should be exposed gradually to the world is disappearing." Crow pointed out that the children on television now acted less like kids than like tiny adults. Even the notion that there were certain words adults shouldn't use around their children—swear words, as we used to say—had become "faintly ridiculous."

But perhaps the truth lies a few steps past Postman and Crow. Perhaps, in a weird way, children knew more than adults, or were at least better able to articulate it. We can remember our exhilaration at seeing *The Bad News Bears* for the first time—these kids said "shit" and "ass" just like we did. (They weren't allowed to say "fuck" yet, however. First film use by a minor?—1976, probably, in *Taxi Driver*. First film use by a minor who wasn't a child prostitute?—1980, *Foxes.*) It felt like life. We can also remember the first time, the weird first time, our parents asked our opinion, or our advice. This happened often, of course, on *One Day at a Time,* but it was strange to have it in our own homes. The smart-mouthed kid became a stock character in films—Alfred Lutter in *Alice Doesn't Live Here Anymore* may be the ground zero of this phenomenon, but there were also *Bugsy Malone, A Little Romance, Little Darlings,* et cetera.

It was all over TV in the eighties. *Diff'rent Strokes. The Facts of Life. Family Ties.* Child characters who were swifter than their adult minders. Adultified children or miniature adults—characters who, in the words of one critic, "possess the tastes, mores, sensibility, knowledge and even cynicism that until recent years were the exclusive province of maturity." The tone of the shows could best be summed up by a 1982 NBC press release for the program *Silver Spoons.* "Ricky helps Edward to be an adult, and Edward teaches his son the pleasures of childhood." This was an era in which Michael J. Fox would offer fatherly advice to his TV father Michael Gross and then ask, mock threateningly, "This won't happen again, will it?" (Answers Dad, "We're both getting older. One of us is bound to grow up sooner or later.") In earlier sentimental shows, kids were sought out for their *innocence*—they were untainted by the world, so their opinions might offer adults a fresh take on things. In the seventies, children were sought out for *worldliness*—they were tougher about the world, because they'd seen more of it on the tube. As one programmer defended the shows, "I think television has served a very useful function in helping kids to realize [that] the age of innocence is gone." *The New York Times* summarized the changes in an article title from the era: "Junior Knows Best: TV's View of Children Today."

"It was like nobody wanted you to be a kid anymore," a young man named Peter Richman told us. "That wasn't enough. You were supposed to be precocious now. I mean, I don't know what childhood was like for my parents. But when I would see reruns from the fifties, I couldn't bear the kids. They didn't *do* anything. They were totally at the mercy of what happened around them. I remember watching Tatum O'Neal in *Paper Moon*. She was the only person who knew what was going on in that whole movie. You wanted to be like that—grow up *fast*. There was an article in *Newsweek* in the early eighties about teenage sex. It was supposed to be depressing—kids are experimenting too young, blah blah blah. But what I remember is racing through it in the supermarket to find a graph. I wanted to see if I was ahead or behind."

A strange era, the seventies. In 1975, William Gaddis won the National Book Award for a novel, *J.R.*, about a stock tycoon who is actually a twelve-year-old boy. The idea was in the air, to grow up and be an adult as quickly as possible. That way, you could stop being a burden and start being an ally to your folks. For us, the attraction was to stop being dependent and more or less get *away* from our folks, who seemed to have enough troubles of their own. In this era, the idea that you could learn all you needed to about the modern world from television began popping up. David Bowie, the extraterrestrial in 1976's *The Man Who Fell to Earth,* learns all he needs to about earthly culture from watching television, and it devastates him. He becomes, in the final shot, a celebrity, a figure of glamorous suffering, which is what celebrities are. We feel with them their great anxieties over their new film releases. We feel their heartaches over their failing marriages. We feel their fresh excitement at their new honeymoons. The gardener-savant in Jerzy Kosinski's *Being There* (played by Peter Sellers in the film version) impresses everyone with random epigrams from television, and at the end of *that* film seems chillingly on his way to becoming president. This notion was picked up as burlesque by Hollywood and TV. Robin Williams as Mork is an anthology of old television attitudes. The robot in *Short Circuit* cheerfully learns about "being a guy" from a total immersion in TV, as does the green visitor in *E.T.*, as does the mermaid in *Splash,* as do the aliens in *Explorers,* as does the unfrozen Neanderthal in *Encino Man.* We lumber to the set as clods and emerge as socialized adults. It's true. This may have explained the idea, early in the cycle, that kids knew more than their elders. They had all day to watch television. To pick up people-handling from *Donahue* (we're all different—but okay), to learn about love from Valerie Harper and Mary Tyler Moore. Parents spent all day working—they didn't have time, spending all day in the real world, to learn about the real world the way their kids did. Thus, the child savant.

Certain behaviors separate adults from children. Adults hold jobs. Adults have access to sex. The age you crossed those boundaries, and got at those goodies, plummeted in the seventies and eighties. By the mid-eighties, studies reported the majority of eleventh graders were having sex "regularly." Three quarters of us used alcohol once a week (and the inclusion of *this* stat seems as antiquated as the notion of inappropriate words did to Postman). When a professor of economics at USC mounted a national survey of high school seniors, he was "startled" to discover that 80 percent of them held jobs. Around half of the group worked sixteen hours or more; one tenth worked more than thirty hours a week. Said the professor, "Teens are experiencing the same pressures as working mothers: trying to hold school lives, work lives and home lives together." As the editor of the annual *Who's Who Among American High School Students* explained, "twenty years ago, we would have looked at the things today's 'popular' kids are doing, and we would have said, 'Those are not nice kids.' " One twenty-eight-year veteran of the Los Angeles elementary school system asked the *Los Angeles Times* the pertinent question, and then went on to answer it. "What happened to childhood? I'll tell you what happened. Children are skipping it."

As psychologist David Elkind, the author of 1981's *The Hurried Child,* told the *Chicago Tribune* in 1988, "The things I wrote about have not disappeared but have in fact become entrenched." How entrenched? In 1924, a group of mothers in an Indiana town were asked to name the qualities they thought were most important in their children. The answers have a distinctly twenties ring: "Conformity and strict obedience." Half a century later, researchers went back to the same Indiana town, and asked modern mothers what the most important qualities in their kids were. Their answer: "Autonomy and independence."

Autonomy and independence. That was childhood—and we haven't begun to talk about divorce yet. Some of what happened—and we should never forget this—was a direct response to older child-rearing methods. It was a sincere attempt to do well by us. Our parents asked themselves if their childhoods of "conformity and strict obedience" had really paid off in the end. Our parents based their new decisions on their own experience. It hadn't left them especially well-prepared for the world—"autonomy and independence," telling your kids they were on their own from the start, might better equip us for where the country was headed.

What the nineties tell us, on one level, is that the country feels this was a failed experiment, too. The childhoods of the newest kids (who will have more or less the same toddlerhoods we did) will be a direct response to what worked and what didn't work in our own youths.

Already, there are campaigns to limit violence on television (old *Kojak* and *Mannix* episodes, discovered late at night on cable, seem anachronistically bloody), and there is a spooky concern with "role models." National articles get written about whether Bart Simpson is a good role model, whether *Beavis and Butt-Head* send viewers the "wrong message." (MTV obediently shifted the program from seven P.M. to ten-thirty, forgetting that most kids have access to VCRs.) Congress conducts hearings, actual hearings, over whether Sega video games go too far. It's sentimental, of course—trying to draw boundaries around what we can control, as a way of staring down the things we can't. When *Jurassic Park* was released in 1993, there were TV news reports discussing whether the film was "too frightening" for preteens.

It is hard to express how ridiculous this sounds to anyone who grew up in the seventies and eighties. In the eighties, there was one video game, Death Race 2000, in which contestants drove dune buggies after fleeing little video stick figures. When you caught one, when you rolled over one, it turned into a cross. The machine merrily played "Taps," and you got a point. In the seventies, when Spielberg's *Jaws* came out, you went to see it at your own risk. If the big mechanical shark spoiled your summer, that was your own fault. It would probably toughen you up, too. In the clamor over "role models," it's hard not to remember films like 1977's PG-rated *The Little Girl Who Lives Down the Lane.* In that film, Jodie Foster plays a thirteen-year-old girl living completely on her own. Her mother has gone, her father has died. She pays her own bills, cooks her own food. She even conducts—at age thirteen—an active sexual relationship with a young local magician. (This was entrancing for the thirteen-year-olds we were then.) The movie has a happy ending. The town sheriff—a lecherous fatso—is all set to expose Jodie's unorthodox style of living when a big plank falls on his head. Jodie and the magician make him disappear, by burying him in the basement. It isn't the *plot* of the film that's especially interesting (though it's amusing to guess what nineties parent groups would make of the film were it released today). What's interesting is that, in the climate of the times, the film was regarded as nothing special. Jodie was yet another hard-edged kid making it on her own. She was autonomous and independent. Anyway, it was a part she'd played many times before.

And for all the noise about values—change the things you can, ignore the things you can't—the economic facts of the matter have made the new childhood a fixture. By the early nineties, newspapers like the *Atlanta Journal-Constitution* could publish cheerful articles with titles like this: "The Kids Take Over: The Child of the 90s Cleans the House, Looks After Siblings, and Does the Grocery Shopping While Mom and Dad Are at Work." The paper likened these new kids to Hazel—the lead character of a fifties sitcom about a maid. There had been "such rapid social changes in the past two decades" that children now fulfilled a whole new set of demands—they organized carpools, cooked, changed diapers. One "expert in children" from Texas A&M even invented a special new word for it. The nineties family was a "filiarchy." The child was in charge. He explained, "As we saw two parents go to work in the seventies and eighties, there was just simply a need on the part of the parents for the children to play a different role." You wouldn't necessarily say, in the last twenty years, that family life had gone to the dogs. You would say that family life has consisted of kids going to *feed* the dogs—and their brothers and sisters—and to the market to buy food, and to the subway station to pick up their parents, plus to an after-school job to provide their own pocket change. (An imaginary scene from a forties movie: "Daddy, I want a *pony*." "All right, but you'll have to take care of it." An imaginary scene from a nineties movie: "All right, but you'll have to drive to the country to pick it out, check the breeding papers, arrange for the rental of one of those big trailers to get it home, go to the vet, and call the municipality about arranging the permit.") None of these changes are inherently bad. But you would have to say that many of the essential differences between children and adults had been eliminated. There goes Postman's "Childhood" bus, moving at a pretty good clip, just shrinking out of visual range.

ii.
"after the split,
I felt like I was wearing
a thousand hats.
in one day
I could be a college student,
my mother's therapist,
my dad's escort
and my brother's mother.
small wonder I was
a little ditzy that year."
—*a twenty-four-year-old quoted in* The New York
Times Magazine, *February 1990*

And then we get to divorce, which made a radical situation more radical still. Stop and look, for a second. You thought we were carping, up above, when we talked about the *Hazel* kids, didn't you? If you're older than we are. Stop and think. In America, there are so many inducements not to stop and think, an unpleasant thought is like a guy asking you for change in the middle of the sidewalk. Brush on by. But think about your own childhoods. Compare the *Hazel* story with Jodie Foster. Twenty years ago, in the mid-seventies, it was considered "news" if a little girl took care of just *herself.* That was enough news to give you the plot of a movie. What would you have thought, in the sixties, in the fifties, of a high school classmate with a schedule like that? You would have thought—the drudgery of the poor. You would have thought, before you turned your eyes back to your own notebook, or your cheerful friends—that poor farm kid. With all that crap to do, he or she doesn't stand a chance. That life would have filled your attention for an alarmed second, and then you would have turned away. That, after all—taking care of kids, cooking for them, shopping, earning money—is the chore list of the house-trailer daughter in *To Kill a Mockingbird.* It's such a drag that Tom Robinson commits the unpardonable Deep South crime of feeling sympathy for a white person.

Now think about this for a second. As humans, our great talent is for getting used to things. It's a surprise—and then we get used to it. Our brains are like water buckets, and every new surprise we pour into them makes some other old surprise dribble over the side. For most of the country's history, kids had two parents. Just like that. You had two parents, and you grew up, and then you got married and your own kids had two parents. That was just one of the plus normal things. Everyone in your high school classes—we know this from statistics—everyone but maybe two or three kids had married parents. Now, twenty years later, only *half* the kids have parents married to each other. Ten years from now, only a *third* of the kids will.

Don't take our word for it. There are numbers. In 1977, *Newsweek* reported in a concerned cover story that one in three marriages were ending in divorce. Fifteen years later, that number was one marriage in two. Since 1976, the country has averaged one million divorces a year—that's a lot of divorces. Throughout the fifties, more than 80 percent of all kids were raised "in families with two biological parents who were married to each other." That meant less than two of your ten friends, in those fifties classrooms, had parents who were separated. For us, the odds were just as good that the kids we knew would have divorced parents as that they would not.

There are hundreds of these numbers. The point is to show how big the shift was, how different childhood is now from the way most Americans had been raised. The number of "latchkey kids" tripled during the seventies—in fact, the term was rarely used before the eighties. You thought it might mean that kids had to lock themselves in during the afternoons—guides for the new situation suggested youngsters "close first-floor curtains" so that passersby could not tell they were alone, not answer the door ("if it's important, that person will come back later"), and never enter their after-school homes if the door was already open ("unless you know your parents are home early"). According to the *Better Homes and Gardens* book *Your Child: The Latchkey Years,* the term refers to the keys such kids wear on strings around their necks. A gruesome image. As of the mid-eighties, children living with a husband and wife as parents made up only 28 percent of all households. The proportion who lived with their two *biological* parents made up only 12 percent. Those of us who lived with only a single parent doubled, from 10 percent in 1970 to more than 20 percent in 1980—and those of us living with only our moms saw our living standard, according to a 1992 study, drop by 33 percent. Other effects? A 1988 study by the National Center for Health Statistics showed that children of divorce—again, half the people our age—were "two to three times as likely as children in two-parent families to have emotional and behavioral problems."

Those are the numbers. Ellen Goodman—that warmhearted columnist—referred to what happened in the seventies and eighties as "a national divorce experiment" whose full results would only be tabulated later, after people our age were all grown up. Well, we're becoming adults now, and the precincts have already begun reporting.

If the divorce wave had occurred during the fifties, when there was more money in the country, it wouldn't have been as bad. Our mothers would have stayed home, lived on alimony, and done the things mothers usually did, only without the fathers present. They would have been old doubles partners learning the singles game, and staying on their side of the court. But having it happen in the seventies, when the economic squeeze also happened, meant that kids would have to take care of themselves and their younger brothers. It meant we would have even *less* of a childhood. It meant kids in some cases would have to take care of their parents—what a psychiatrist in *The New York Times* called "a proxy situation." One young woman wrote to that publication in 1990 and said, "At my father's wedding, I gave a toast. I said that his wedding day was the last day of a job for me—a job that I was happy to hand over to his new wife. I explained how I had been confidante, wife and daughter, and that I was looking forward to being just his daughter. Everybody laughed, but it wasn't funny."

What does it mean to have your parents divorce? The first thing you learn is that your parents are other people, more or less just like you. You learn about money, of course—your mother asks you to make sure your father has sent the child support check, and arms you with a nightmare bill story to make sure the money comes quick. The third thing you learn is what their value is to the culture. You learn that they may not be able to get more money from their jobs. You learn that they might not be the most attractive people in the world—that other single men or women might not be thrilled to date them. A strange thing to think about. You learn they don't have, as they say, all the answers. When your parents aren't divorced, you *think* they have all the answers. But that's because they aren't being asked that many questions. Or the hard questions, anyway. When they're married, it's all the *same* questions. Divorced, you see them as people, with certain kinds of tastes in men or women, with certain kinds of habits. And because there isn't another person there, they seek you out. There's this human thing, about sharing your impressions with someone. About knowing someone cares about problems you're having, thoughts you're having. This need is usually filled by having a married person right there: They become your study partner for life. When one side of the couple goes away, that need remains. As children we filled it. So you ended up being one kind of friend for your schoolmates—talking about bionics, about girls in the class, about weekend activities. And you were another kind of friend for your parents—helping them judge the parade of possible life-mates, checking in with their day at work, talking about what bills they might and might not have to pay. That more than television, finally, adults you right up. There aren't that many surprises in the world after your father explains to you the trouble he's having finding a date Saturday night.

Many people we spoke with, children of divorce or children of "continuously intact families" (our national lexicon responding to the need for another new term), discussed how the divorce-time affected their own relationships. The truism, of course—and it was borne out for us—is that young people whose parents split up would not "want to put my own kids through that." It speaks, certainly, to just what they made of the situation. It was painful enough that they wouldn't want to repeat it. Most wanted their kids to have more "traditional" upbringings than they had, whether this was economically feasible or not. One young man was very emphatic in speaking of the difficulties when people whose parents stayed together become romantic with people whose parents did not. This young man spoke of the varying "expectations" each side brings to the relationship. For the two had been told conflicting bedtime stories, in a sense, and went into a romance with conflicting morals to the story of wedded love. "It's very different. You think you were moving on one track—*towards* something—and it turned out they were moving on another. An institution that was positive to you was only negative for them. I'd like to say I would only date somebody whose parents stayed together. But there aren't that many people like that out there."

What we have to remember is that the solution is not to stick in a marriage. This was a point a number of people made, the important point. The idea is to wait before marriage until you can find someone to stick with. It's important to remember that every generation's behavior is the result of years of a sort of informal Research and Development. Our parents had seen their parents plug it out in marriages no matter what, for the sake of the children. They didn't feel particularly gratified by it. By the lights of their experience, it *wasn't* better for the children if incompatible people stayed together. Their lives proved it. And so they tried the opposite. We now know that it's also not great for kids if their parents split up. But the experiment had to be tried, and now the question has been answered. Neither response to the question of families works terribly well. Thus our response, which will work as R and D for those robot-raised kids in the next century. But it is silly to ignore all the free research, the free data. Staying married didn't work. Divorcing doesn't much work. Thanks for the tips.

Elizabeth Sherrill works as a journalist in Chicago—her parents divorced when she was six. She was raised by her mother. "We had these people who didn't mean to have us, who got stuck with us. I mean, my mother just wasn't equipped for the world she ended up living in. She was equipped to be a housewife in the suburbs. Instead she's a single mother in Chicago, in a world she didn't plan on, and she just wants to keep a spic and span home. I mean, everything was conflicted, you know? Things didn't work out the way she planned. Because there was an explosion in this whole country. The baby boom, they have kids, they've got a plan, they've got some value system they picked up along the way. Whether you think it's a good value system or not, any value system is good enough for kids. But the problem is that my mother had value system interruptus. I mean I swear to you, she's *still* waiting for a husband and a house in the suburbs. I mean not really, but she never came to terms with the life she ended up with."

When asked how big the divorce's effect was, Elizabeth said, "I think it had an effect on my whole life. I mean—well,

I don't have that many examples of happy marriage, do I? Recently, I've seen some people get married. And I've thought, for the first time, This looks like something I could do, because I'm having the first examples of people who look like they're making a reasonable decision. I mean, the role models I've had have been *disastrous*. My mother and my father—getting married ruined their lives."

On the other hand, she had no doubts divorcing was the right choice. "I found my parents' divorce painful. But that doesn't mean I would have found them together any *less* painful. It wasn't that they got divorced. It was the fact that they got married as if sleepwalking into it. I mean, they sleepwalked their way into everything. It was just the thing to do. You got married, you had kids. Now, people have to make conscious decisions. You have to live a conscious life. It's better."

Elizabeth has mixed feelings about growing up in the seventies and eighties. She felt it was "a hard time to come of age." On the other hand, "I think it's going to ultimately be for the good of families and people in general. Because ultimately I think families will be better structured. There will be different kinds of families that *work,* as opposed to what we have now, which was one kind of family that *didn't* work. But I think we are the eggs that got cracked to make the omelette."

Her own children? "My kids are going to be really boring, I know. I think they're going to have an easy life. I'm interesting because I had a hard life. But I think having an easy life is probably more important than being interesting."

You can hear in Elizabeth's last answer the whir of the bus pulling away. She remembers—from the TV shows of the late sixties, from the early years of her toddlerhood—what childhood was supposed to be like. Her own childhood was not that way. As she told us, "When I was a teenager, I was such a sophisticated little thing. I just remember a lot of responsibilities in high school. Everything was reversed. I was such a little adult. You know, for most of my life before the age of eighteen, I had to take care of my mom, I had jobs, I had a sense that I had to do very well in school to get into a good college and get out of this miserable life we were leading. I was so responsible and so on top of things." That was the life most of us were prepared for by childhood. And that's of course another great irony. If you had pulled aside some social observer, taken them out of the action and asked them to make a prediction, would they have guessed how long most of us would spend in adolescence *after* we left our parents?

This was part of the great press buildup before the 1990s: We had had these hard childhoods, where we'd been asked to mature awfully quickly. We weren't going to come into the world with a lot of illusions about picking the right job and trying to live softly. We were going to be materialists: As David Leavitt—yet another child of divorce—wrote in his *Esquire* essay, "We trust ourselves and money, period." When eighties psychologists were frightened about our materialism—at least until the material went away, so you couldn't be a materialist anymore—this was what frightened them. We had learned some ugly things in childhood, things that you weren't supposed to learn until you were out of college—that the world is mostly about cash, that cash is the first step, the admission ticket, to almost everything. Postman worried that the "charm, innocence, and malleability" of childhood had been pounded out of us, and a lot of us were proud of it. We knew more. We had gone through our childhoods faster—we would go through our early adulthood faster, too. In our surveys and interviews, almost no one said they were where they'd imagined they would be when they were teens. We had wanted to get it all over with fast. Postman was *right*. Childhood in the seventies was not an innocent time.

That was what was surprising, so stunning, when people began looking for reasons why so many of us weren't getting to where we wanted to go. One psychologist told the *Los Angeles Times*, "[Eighties] kids were left with the impression that they could have whatever they wanted. Many of them don't know the benefit of struggling. Even though their parents didn't themselves grow up expecting life to be easy, they've inadvertently reinforced that in their kids." It had almost nothing to do with the way childhood was experienced in the 1980s. You couldn't have grown up in the last two decades and expected life to be "easy." When Susan Littwin, in her 1986 book *The Postponed Generation*, described our childhoods, one had to feel one was reading about another culture. We had been raised, she wrote, to be "young Romanovs." We had been given "everything." Our folks had been not absent, or consumed with problems of their own. According to Littwin, they had been "professional parents," utterly absorbed with our fates and welfares. It certainly sounds nice. And you could certainly see how someone with that upbringing could have a little trouble—would need a helping hand—with living in the last quarter of the twentieth century. But nobody who was born after 1960—except for the very rich, who of course weren't having these problems anyway—ever *had* that kind of upbringing in the last quarter of the twentieth century.

Littwin wrote, "The idea that life ought to be easy is especially popular among today's young adults. Parents, for their part, are honestly stunned. It never dawned on them that when they gave their children everything, they were withholding independence." You could see how that could be true, and it sounds like a plausible formulation, so far as it goes. (It sounds like a sweet deal, too.) But it would have to be true of some other decade, or some other country. Independence had been ours from the very start, and while none of us would argue against someone wanting to give us everything now—it is not what happened *then*.

The sociologist David Reisman asked in 1951, "How is it that every society gets, more or less, the social character it needs?" We became what the society needed—and that's fine, it left us better prepared for the society we were going to live in. The society *needed* kids who would be able to take care of themselves (and others). The society needed kids who hadn't bulked up on misperceptions about the world—the society needed lean kids who could accept and incorporate cold facts quickly. The society, in the seventies and eighties, needed kids who could grow up *fast,* because their parents and the society no longer had time for kids who were going to try to do it at any other pace. At the age of eighteen, we had more or less accepted this proposition. We were responsible for ourselves. We were doing our burdened parents a favor by staying out of their hair. The society needed kids who weren't going to wait around, and this is what we trained ourselves not to do. The pain for us, for children raised in the seventies and eighties, is that society's needs changed midstream. We have to be patient, now. We have to wait to be adults until the society has more places for adults—the society now has more adults than places. It was a midcourse reversal. And it was painful for us, for our self-image, because as those Indiana mothers said in the second survey, what was important for us as kids was autonomy and independence. Those were the things we were trained to respect. It made it a bit harder to respect ourselves when society now tried to find a new pace for us to live at.

# iv.
# indentured students

"*I fortunately only have a ten-thousand-dollar debt. I know others who have forty-thousand-dollar loans. My parents are helping me out. I feel horribly guilty, but I haven't made more than five thousand dollars in one year since I have been out of school. It is very difficult to enter life with a debt. If you can't find a good job right away you can't pay the bills, which leads to bad credit. Then you can't get an apartment, car, or home, and you end up living at home again. It's a catch-22, a vicious circle.*"

—*Katie Barron, Norfolk, Virginia, twenty-four*

## "a more sophisticated vehicle"
### —*James Vebber, 1992*

This is another money chapter. If you attended college, and you're several thousand dollars in debt, you'd probably like to find out how it happened. (The *average* is about ten thousand dollars of debt for all college graduates, though of course if you went to private schools it's probably higher. If you went on to get a graduate degree, it's higher still; your debt reads like the Atlantic City tab of some new arrival at Gambler's Anonymous.) If you're the parent of a kid who's deep in debt—if you're the parent of a kid who is probably deeper in debt than you are, although she's half your age— you might also like to find out how it happened. If you're not in debt at all for your education, this chapter should be a breeze. It should be a little like reading, the next morning, about the crash of an airplane you failed to board.

The years of cheap educations—we missed those too. We came into the system just as high school graduates started to get squeezed out of the economy (an average college graduate now earns about twice as much as an average high school graduate), so we didn't much have a choice about going to college. Not that anything was going to stop us from going anyway. College was the big glamorous ball for our generation. It was the tuxedo-and-top-hat time. You filled out your applications, and then you pulled your cuffs down from inside your jacket, buffed the sheen of your hat on your wrist, adjusted your cummerbund. We'd been adults so long, perfecting our adult act so long—but we'd been living with our folks. We had great taste in furnishings, clothing, music, food, but we were stuck living in our parents' houses, wearing clothes they liked, keeping our slick music low and eating what our parents wanted us to. We had better taste than our families did. We were hipper, we were adult—and now we were going to be independent. Now we'd get a chance to show what we could do on our own. College is in many ways as good as it got for some of us. For we've had to give up our taste in furnishings since then, in clothes and in food, as we've progressed into our middle twenties. (Music is how we express suavity now—liking the right sorts of music. It's still cheap enough so you can manage to make a statement with it, unlike the rest. You can express a great deal of unbowed sophistication, even if your cash situation is pretty shaky, by getting hold of the right music.) Now we understand why our parents had such lesser tastes than we did. They couldn't afford them. We can't afford them either.

Nor could they afford college for us. That was all right. We would have signed whatever it took to get in. And we did. We came out of our teenagerhoods with the necessary social character pretty well formed. Society had the character it needed, at least as far as tuitions were concerned. It didn't surprise us that we were going to have to assume large debts to get into school. That was more of the same. There'd been that cheap college time—average private college fees were two thousand dollars a year in 1967; they were ten thousand a year by 1980—and that was gone. We'd missed that. There'd been a time when parents mostly paid for their kid's tuitions—and when they couldn't, they took on the loans. But we'd missed that, too. It wasn't a surprise, exactly. We'd been prepared for it. We'd been pulling our weight for a pretty long time as it was. Who can say what our parents thought as we signed documents every year, promising to repay such and such a loan at such and such a rate beginning on such and such month? Probably they were as relieved as we that the money was available in some form to get us there. And by the mid-eighties, the country was on its roll. It didn't seem implausible that, what with high salaries and a few months of economizing, we might get the whole sum paid back in a single year.

See, our timing here was doubly off. Colleges had expanded like crazy to meet the size-challenge of the baby boom. There had been all those young people coming in, every year. They stretched the colleges out, got them building new dorms and new classrooms. And then the boom was over, and there we were, poised over the colleges, a storm cloud too tiny to provide all the irrigation those thirsty schools were going to need. And then, secondly, the government changed the rules about how college was paid for. Loans were suddenly available for almost everyone. So the schools began admitting lots of us—making the degree a little less valuable than it would have been, erasing some of that small-size advantage we were supposed to gain—and they realized they could charge us a heap to do it. The colleges charged more, and our degrees promised to earn less. But we're getting ahead of ourselves.

# Late Bloomers

This is a money story, and most of us are bored by money stories. In prose, one of the most inelegant characters is the slashed "$" sign. It's a signal to the eye: Skip ahead. Here comes a dollar figure. But actually, money stories are fascinating. And this one particularly so. Like reading a medical book—the *Merck Manual*—if you're a hypochondriac. Ah, *here's* why. *This* is why I have that symptom. Of course, it's perfectly natural. This money story is about why so many of us owe so much money for college.


How much did our tuitions increase? We have the sense they kept getting higher, but it's hard to find something to compare them to. Anyway, all that seemed to matter was filling out the Financial Aid Form each spring, mailing it to New Jersey before the end of March, hoping the figures would tally up. All that mattered was getting a loan from the GSL people. But the tuition jump was extreme. Compare it to something like a car—since college is for people our age, compare it with a car for people our age—and you see the size of the increase.

The Mustang has always been Ford's young-guy automobile. It fell out of favor in the mid-eighties, when you mostly saw it at rental companies. You'd go to rent a subcompact, and here would be this snubbed, boxy white vehicle, which looked like a big Reebok shoe. You'd walk to the front, see the name, and think "*This* is what happened to the Mustang. Wow." In the early nineties, Ford decided to retool the thing—spruce it up, make it irresistible to people our age. They added new features, filmed an MTVish ad. It's a hip-looking car now. It's for us, like college was. In 1970, the Mustang retailed for $2,721. By 1994, the Mustang was retailing for a little over $11,000. When we telephoned James

112

Vebber, a public affairs representative at Ford, he was testy and apologetic and defensive about the rise in price. He kept wanting to account for it. "You have to remember," he said, "there is a heck of a lot more equipment on these cars now than then. We've kept on adding technologies. Dual air bags and whatnot. It's a much more sophisticated vehicle than it was in 1970."

In 1970, total annual costs for the average Ivy League college were $3,000. The Mustang cost $2,721. They started the race from the same gate. For academic year 1993–94, total average costs are $25,000. There is no James Vebber at these schools to tell us that there is a heck of a lot more equipment in the university education of 1993 than there was in 1970. Class sizes are a little bigger; more courses are taught by TAs. In fact, by the early 1990s, experts in places like *Rolling Stone* and *USA Today* were frequently comparing the "value" of a college degree to the value of a high school diploma in the seventies. It was the basic thing you needed to enter the economy; it was no longer anything special. But for the Mustang to have kept pace with the price it's market share was paying for education, it would now have to cost almost $23,000. If you went into a Ford showroom, and the dealer told you the Mustang was now a $23,000-dollar car, you'd laugh, or snort in disbelief. It's a nice $11,000 car. But none of us could really snort at the tuition prices. We didn't have *time*. We just wanted it paid up, regardless of how much we were going to pay later.

It's a proposition generally agreed to that wages in the U.S. have been stagnant since the early seventies. So if tuition prices shot up at the same time the wages of our parents were standing still, you had an immediate problem. Who was going to make up the shortfall? If nothing else had happened—had there been no change in college funding—either everyone would have been out of luck, or everyone would have been *in* luck. Colleges would have had to keep a lid on tuitions. Young students would not have had to engage in heavy borrowing. But we know this is not what happened. So where did the extra money come from?

## ii.

## "slavery is no longer permitted, [but] even the idea of 'indentured students' should not be dismissed."

*—Katherine Hanson, executive director,*
*Consortium on Financing Higher Education, 1986*

Edward B. Fiske, then education editor at *The New York Times,* wrote in 1986, "Strange as it may seem, the concept of borrowing for college is relatively new. Up through the 1950s, most [middle-class] families paid for their children's education through savings and current income. Students were able to help out by working after school and during vacations." Scholarships were available—on a merit basis—but borrowing on a large scale for college had never been attempted. By 1986, however, Fiske could write something very different. "Credit," he said, "is the new lubricant of American higher education."

There is a reason the concept is new. The GSL—the most popular loan, the Whopper of the federal system—was not even available until the middle sixties. President Johnson began the program in 1965. It was meant to be a little stopgap for lower-income families. Parents could borrow, in the fall let's say, a small·tide-the-student-over sum; they would repay in the spring. The government would pick up the interest on such loans in the interim. Johnson did not foresee national banks administering a major program; it was meant to be minor, and local. Although much else by the middle sixties was loosening, eligibility requirements for the GSL remained a bulwark of stability. You had to earn less than twelve thousand dollars a year. You had to prove you really needed the money, before government stepped in and saw to it that you no longer needed the money. Nor had Johnson ever intended to involve the government in the middle-income college finance racket—until the middle sixties, most aid had been targeted at the poor, in the form of work-study and grants.

For its first decade, the program stayed small. By 1977, only six million students had taken advantage of it; they had borrowed around ten billion bucks. Most aid remained in its old form: For academic year 1976–77, 80 percent of all government money was released to students as grants and work-study; 20 percent was released as loans. Then President Carter changed the eligibility rules. Then everything else changed, too.

Colleges hate it if you say this. If you want to see just how many separate muscles there are in a financial aid officer's face, or a university public relations officer's face, and you want to see how quickly those muscles can move, try bringing this up. But the jump in prices came *after* the loans. Any graph will show you that. You have a steady slope until around 1978—a tough grade, but still relatively climbable. Then, in 1978, the new loan program kicked in, and the graphs start looking like Everest.

Why 1978? There'd been the oil inflation from 1973 to 75. College costs had risen with that inflation—not ahead of it; college costs wouldn't really hit their stride until the late seventies—and middle-class parents were having tough times meeting the bill. Middle-class loans were a hot topic in 1978's Ninety-fifth Congress—so hot that the changed policy, the Middle Income Student Assistance Act, was debated for months and finally produced on the last day of the session. It was signed into law immediately by President Carter. The new act basically removed all restrictions on federal loans. Before, there had been those income tests; now, there were no income tests at all, and a Kennedy kid would have just as easy a time qualifying as a Katzenjammer Kid. Not everyone was enchanted by the idea. As *Fortune* magazine warned in December of 1978, "Our own view is that the new act is bad news. [It] will have the effect of raising the cost of education. Anything that makes it easier to pay tuition bills will also make it easier to raise tuition charges. Ultimately, the legislation will subsidize the educational establishment rather than your kids."

*Fortune* was right. The problem with making the loans so easily available was that it removed incentive for keeping costs down from the system. Had there been no way to get more money, colleges couldn't have asked for more money. There's a famous story about Thomas Schelling, a Harvard economist who travels a lot. When Schelling arrives at a hotel, he always offers to pay extra for a room without a television. There are rarely such rooms. Schelling would *like* to work in his room—but he knows if the television is there, this will be impossible, because he will watch it. Similarly, once the money was out there, it was not going to be long before colleges started asking us to get our hands on it. It introduced the standard lover's gambit to college finance. The willingness to take on debt became almost a measure of how committed we were to education. It became our lover's sacrifice.

How fast did rates rise? In 1978—the last year before the changeover—college costs rose 4 percent. That's it. That *was* the rate of inflation. By 1981, college prices were rising at around 10 percent a year. This was *twice* the rate of inflation. (Which, although rising by one point, was still moving at its turtle's pace of 5 percent a year.) College costs diligently doubled the inflation rate almost every year of the eighties. By the mid-eighties, private college tuitions were twelve grand a year. By 1989, they were twenty grand a year. University officials kept trying to account for the rises with various laudable explanations. The salaries of professors had not risen for many years, and there was to be a one-time catching-up period. (*Time,* 1985.) All those old buildings needed to be fixed up—"The ivy covered up a whole lot, quite literally." (*U.S. News & World Report,* 1985.) You had to add computers. (*Fortune,* 1985; in the same article, reporters found that tuition prices were *five* times higher than they had been at both public and private universities in the late 1960s.) Most lamely, utilities had raised their rates. (*Newsweek,* 1985.)

So it was all the electricity that was making costs rise. And you couldn't have chunks of plaster falling on students' heads. Nor did you want to lose professors to "industry" (though how you can lose a history professor, or a philosophy professor, to industry is difficult to imagine, and anyway, salaries for professors never *did* catch up to inflation, despite the price hikes). In 1992, after it was all over, and extraordinary tuitions had lost their capacity to surprise, *Time* offered the most reasonable explanation. They offered it with a maddening tone of fait accompli: "Tuition was one cash cow that universities could keep milking through the eighties." Direct federal funding to schools had dried up, and so had endowments. The only way to keep pace with their spending during the baby boom had been to raise tuition. No more complex than that. Universities had been pressed to seek out more students, from a smaller pool. In many cases, tuitions had gone up to cover the costs of financial aid for those students—whose expenses kept going up, because of the raised tuitions.

With tuitions soaring, there was going to be a problem in handling the increases. The change in loan policy allowed the *students,* kids, to subsidize the increases. We had agreed—we agreed each time we signed the yearly GSL form—to pay for our own educations after the fact. This was simply another change in the way things had usually been done—this was the Disappearance of Paternalism. William McPherson, a senior fellow at the Brookings Institute, saw this as a great shift in the social contract between the generations, a "tricky intergenerational question." He asked, "Is it right that a couple whose parents paid for their education may now want their children to pay for their own?" Theodore Marchese, of the American Association for Higher Education, put the question in the clearest possible terms. He laid it on the line. "The rules about paying for college have changed. We've said to young people: 'If you want a higher education, here's a loan. Pay for it yourself.' The message of a loan is, 'Go forward if you want, but on your own nickel.' "

By 1993, about two trillion nickels had been borrowed. In 1978, after thirteen years of the program, a little more than $10 billion had been loaned to students. But with the rate change, this graph started looking like Everest too. It had to—this graph was climbing the previous one. By the early nineties, more than 62 million student loans had been made through the federal government—ten times as many as the 6 million loans in the GSL's first decade. There had been more than $100 billion borrowed. (As of 1993, $64 billion is still un-repaid.) By the nineties, the old proportion of grants to loans had reversed—two thirds of federal funds were made available in the form of loans, only one third in the form of grants. The default rate went up to 11 percent in the mid-eighties—this means that more than one borrower in ten would admit to the government that they could not pay the money back and would suffer the predictable damage to their credit rating. They would never be able to get mortgages, they would have great difficulty securing a car loan. After the mid-eighties, our job market began to collapse, even as the colleges continued to milk that cash cow. By 1993, *U.S. News & World Report* reported a default rate of 22 percent. More than one in every five kids. The average public and private college student now graduated with more than ten thousand dollars of debt—and this was three thousand dollars higher than the official poverty level for a single person. It meant, if you were that average college student, that "downward mobility" was no vague notion you had when you left school. You had literally dropped down a class, immediately. You were starting behind the eight ball. As of 1977, $11.5 billion had been borrowed by students in toto. By the mid-eighties, people our age were borrowing $10 billion every *year*. By the early nineties, we were borrowing $15 billion.

That was the load we carried—and in many cases fumbled, bobbled, and dropped. By 1992, when student defaults hit their high-water mark of $3.6 billion a year (they had cost the country only $200 million in 1980), college loans became an official political problem. They were a mini S & L crisis. Karen Hanson, executive director of the Consortium on Higher Education Financing, had joked in the eighties that, "Slavery is no longer permitted. You can't repossess a student who defaults on a loan." But, on the other hand,

"Even the idea of 'indentured students' should not be dismissed." This joke returned as simple information—in the sad way hyperbole often does—in the early nineties. Representative William Ford told *Money* magazine in 1992, "We have created a new indentured class in the United States— the student debtor." In 1993, President Clinton came up with a solution—the government would make loans directly to students, without the intermediate banks. Lower interest, slower defaults. An experiment had been tried—getting kids to pay for their own colleges through personal bank loans— and it had been a failed experiment. Something new would be whipped together for the next decade. But that was the burden we carried—and continue to carry, more than half of us. That was another bit of R and D we did for the culture— at our own expense—which presumably will be of some benefit to some other generation in the future.

### iii.
### "my future is mortgaged."
*—Joseph Wilson, twenty-two, Georgetown*
*University graduate who owes more than $55,000 in*
*education loans, quoted in* The Washington Post,
*May 1991*

It's easy to imagine why the loan idea made sense in the early eighties. And it's nice to imagine how the people who established the program saw it working. We would borrow around three thousand a year; we'd begin repaying six months after graduation; we'd be finished paying when we hit our early thirties. It must have seemed the best way out of a tight spot.

And it's easy to guess what our parents thought. It's easy, because parents wrote essays about it during the eighties. One of them, John Brandt, writing in *Newsweek,* was a student in the 1950s. "My parents sent me to college and . . . made a lot of sacrifices to do it. . . . All my needs were taken care of. And when I graduated, no debts hung over my head except the debt of gratitude to my parents." But as it turned out, this hadn't been terrific for Brandt—he felt he hadn't worked hard enough in school, because it hadn't been his own dough. Now he wasn't certain he wanted to sacrifice anything so his son could have all his needs met while he went to college. He had decided it was part of the college experience—a very valuable, perhaps even educational, part—to undergo privation while he earned his degree. You almost got the feeling that Brandt thought he was doing his son a favor—along the lines of "This hurts me more than it hurts you."

It was a tricky decade. The colleges had a good deal to fear, about the small baby bust. Sociologists had warned in the late seventies that the smaller pool of young people would result in a lot of colleges closing down. There would be "wrenching reorganization" on the educational level. As late as 1984, business columnist Jane Bryant Quinn wrote in *Newsweek,* "You're seeing the start of what could become a decade of price wars in the ivied halls. A thinning stream of high-school seniors means fewer customers for the bloated educational plant." Colleges would have to "covertly cut the price" or else they would lose students. Newspaper articles from the period have titles like "Weathering the Baby Bust." The way colleges weathered the bust was by admitting most people who applied. In 1970, only 40 percent of all high school seniors went directly to college. By 1987, 53 percent were going. Thus, the price cuts Quinn had forseen in 1984 never came. Instead, universities admitted most applicants and arranged for them to borrow sums to cover the higher costs. This worked for the schools, as *Fortune* had predicted in 1978, but it wasn't great for the students. Although there was a 25 percent drop in the applicant pool, the size of each graduating class continued to rise in the eighties. So the degree cost more, but it was less valuable. A 1990 *Boston Globe* article had the ominously appropriate title, "Colleges Combat Baby Bust." In 1991, a college counselor explained the combat method to *The Washington Post:* "I think there are some students who are getting into schools that wouldn't have taken them in other years. The colleges need the paying customers." So the colleges got through this rough period— and now the size of the classes is expected to rise, in the next century, when the children of the baby boomers begin to apply. The hard time was weathered—those repairs were made, those salaries were raised—and it was done through student loans. The colleges themselves are no longer affected. Only the students.

The banks—well, college loans are their third most profitable loans, you know. Banks make more money on college loans than they do on car loans or mortgages. The "Guaranteed" part of Guaranteed Student Loans means they are guaranteed by the government. If the bank defaults on a student borrower, that bank is repaid in full by the government immediately. So it hasn't been a bad deal for the banks at all. A 1992 congressional study found that many banks were defaulting on students *early,* so eager were they to get their hands on the federal loot. The defaults didn't affect the banks, or the colleges. They only had an effect on taxpayers, and on us.

Nor were the loans enough. *Money* ran a praising article—these kids; the *gumption* they have—in 1986 about the new independent spirit on campus. We were working part-time jobs to pay our way. More than half of all students were working at some after-class job in 1986; more than a quarter were working more than 25 hours a week. This was how we got our extra money together—and of course, it also meant that it now took longer to get through college. By 1987, the average student finished in just over five years. The four-year program was gone. This was attributable to the higher tuition, to the *need* for extra money. But magazines like *American Demographics* and others saw this as an example of "immaturity" in students, that college took them longer. Reporters saw it as new evidence of "indecision." It was of course the *opposite* of immaturity. It was students doing whatever it took to keep themselves at college.

Everyone got what they wanted. Our parents got us through school, catch-as-catch-can. The universities met their payrolls and built a lot of new buildings. The banks got to make their money. Universities survived a difficult time—how? By shifting the difficulty onto us. We got to attend our party.

After college, there were a lot of us looking around at the diminished employment picture, and wondering what was going to happen. Students told newspapers their "futures were mortgaged." (One student wrote an essay in *The Boston Globe* called, "These Days, Diploma Opens Door to Debt, Not Dreams.") But it was a weird kind of debt, a weird kind of mortgage, and in a sense we've had our revenge. The threat has always been that if you didn't repay your loans, you were never going to be fully enrolled in the economy. You were never going to be able to buy certain adult goodies. But a number of people we interviewed told us they never expected to afford those goodies anyway. The threat was toothless. If there wasn't enough money around to pay off college loans—and in many cases there wasn't—then there was probably never going to be enough for houses and cars. As Heléne Bochner, an unemployed history major in Atlanta, Georgia, explained to us, "I've defaulted on my student loans. I mean, how could I pay them? If I had to get a mortgage or something, forget it. The way money is in my life, it's like I'm either going to buy a house in cash or I'm not going to buy a house at all. So I couldn't worry all that much about my credit rating."

The problem—the irony, always the irony—with the loans is that they release you into an eerie world. You get out of college, and you owe ten thousand dollars. Now, in the past, a diligent kid could sock away part of his paycheck every two weeks toward some future purchase. Maybe she could buy a house. Maybe he could buy a car. Now, an average diligent kid is socking away money to pay *backward,* toward a huge purchase already made. They've climbed up a ladder, and now they have to pay for it, rung by rung.

And then of course the desire for a big strike—the small jobs, they don't pay enough if you have to give a good chunk of your paycheck back over to college. They don't pay enough, though they might be the only way to get a shot at the real jobs, with the real money. But they don't pay enough, so you can't take them. You have to keep your options open for a job that will allow you to pay off your debt. If you take a low-paying job, play the game as it's always been played—well, you're going to end up a defaulter, someone inched a little outside the system. Someone who's a problem *within* the system. When college, of course, was the most casual and obedient choice of all.

The coming out of college with a huge debt load—it's strange. It makes things less real for you. It gives you a maverick approach to begin with. If you come out of college owing nothing, you can see the advantages of playing along, of living carefully and tractably inside the margins of the society you've joined. You've got a stake in things. But with a ticking debt clock behind you—you're going to have to begin repayment in six months, in five months, in four months, you're going to have to lie to someone very soon— you feel already *outside* the margins. You're banished. You know, comically, that in a few months you're going to feel a kind of renegade *anyway*. It's hard to take a real pleasure— the impostor's pleasure—in conforming and disappearing into your culture when you know that, by the culture's standards, you're about to become a little bit of a criminal. You're about to become someone who's going to be lying on promissory notes, on unemployment deferments, and on the phone, endlessly lying on the phone. You're going to stop answering the phone, soon, or find someone else to answer it and say you're not there. The women at the banks: they must be lie specialists by now, mustn't they? They must be able to tell by the quickening of the voice, the pause before you tell them how sincerely you're still looking for work (though you've arranged to be paid off the books somewhere else). You're already a scrambler—you're not the straight shooter you might have wanted to be. The irony is that we went to college to get our shot at being normal, at being serious and swanky adults. To play the mature game at its highest level. And to pay for it, you had to become a wheedler—you had to be someone *outside* the mature game from the start, in order to play.

# v.
# musical chairs

"I've always had a good head on my shoulders re-
garding sex. I'm totally adamant about safe sex, and
was even before the real AIDS scare. Because of all
these factors, I'm very selective of who I sleep with.
I'm just careful."

—Molly Jackson, Cincinnati, Ohio, twenty-six

i.

## "some socioeconomic event"
### —*Victor Fuchs,* How We Live, *1983*

You go around thinking that your life is based on a delicate matrix of personal circumstance—you're always ready to explain to someone you meet at a party (where you went hoping to fall in love), how the reason you're this way with romance is because of the way your parents broke up, or the way your first relationship ended painfully. We've made that speech so many times—the evolution of our particular emotional subspecies—that we could put it inside a Valentine's card. The cover would say, in lacy script, *I've Only Just Met You.* Inside, there would be a computer chip that would drone the story of our romantic lives. How many people we loved. Why it didn't work (at the time I thought it was her; really, it was me). The first attempt at living together (you think it's going to be easy, but it's not. It's a whole new situation. My advice now would be not to do it until you're really ready to. Think it over first). The woman you should have married who's married to someone else (I didn't really know what I wanted at age twenty-two. I was looking for too much, I think). Think of the time you'd save, preparing this emotional résumé. Of course, what would you talk about on first dates? It's a drag to give that speech, but it's the only speech we have to give until we establish that shared history with someone, produce the collaborative memories.

All those little concordances—my parents fought over custody so, you know, I have a very hard time leaving people; my first boyfriend, he was really clingy, so if you shoot for too much closeness too soon I'll probably pull away, that's how I am now—they make such embarrassingly tight plot sense. They all so shamelessly *add up*. We give our new lovers our flashbacks so they can understand the present-tense action. It all hangs together. I dated X, so now I am emphatically anti-X (if you want to love me, please try Y). We think we have the whole thing licked—my God, humans aren't so hard to understand after all—and then you read an economist and the whole thing turns out to be economic. As the economist Victor Fuchs puts it, in flawless money-speak, "Without an economic perspective, changes in household living arrangements, fertility, and other social phenomena are often automatically attributed to changing 'norms.' A more careful examination, however, might reveal that the changes are the result of shifts in income or prices." Quite a comedown. All your ex-lovers disappear in a howling flash, all the injustices of your parents' married style, or their divorcing style, shoot up in the same flume, and it turns out it's all money again. It can't be that simple, can it?

Here's Fuchs on where adolescence ends: "More than any other stage of life, adolescence is viewed as a time of transition. Differences in the length of adolescence among and within societies are largely determined by economic factors. The onset of the stage is triggered by biological changes. But the end is usually marked by some socioeconomic event, such as obtaining full-time employment or getting married. The age at which these events occur depends primarily upon the general level of economic development of the society, on the circumstances of the adolescent's parents, and on the adolescent's own prospects for the future."

There you have it. It's chilling to see marriage defined as "some socioeconomic event," but it's hard to argue with the passage. Let's accept as a given that most of us would like to be partnered, married. It's got to be true, hasn't it? You look at movies. You sit down at a movie, and the minute your skin touches the chair and you enter that public dream-state, you realize how simple all the things that people want in a life are. You see how simple it is by how basic the things are for which you start rooting. You want to see the characters end up prosperous. But mostly, you want to see them in love with someone. That's the main thing. You go into a movie and instantly root for them to meet the person they will love. You hope they will be able to swing love from the person they've fastened their attention on. (This assumes you haven't gone to see some film like *Die Hard* or its coevals, in which case you want to see how realistically the effects guys could rig up the blood shots. But then, even in *Die Hard,* you're rooting for Bruce Willis and Bonnie Bedelia to put aside their differences and save their marriage, as we and the scriptwriters know is best.) All the dating we've done—and we've done a whole lot of dating; maybe we've dated more than any generation in history—it's been a screening process. And we've all gone about it with some tender degree of hope. Our lovers start with a perfect score. They start out at a hundred, and their tally starts dropping immediately. We sit there praying they won't disqualify themselves. Pretty soon they get below some cutoff point, and we have to find some-one new. But each time we're hoping this will be, as they say, the person I'll marry. Elizabeth Sherrill, when we asked her to define what being grown-up meant, answered, "It means caring about something more than yourself. Otherwise, it wouldn't be that much different from the life I have now. And then there are kids. That's the biggest thing. I mean, I already earn money, and do all those sorts of things any other grown-up does, so it can't really be that. Because I'm doing all that and I still feel like a kid. So it has to be the caring for somebody else." How different is that, finally, from the socioeconomic event? We must take as a given that we all would *like* to marry. So why aren't we doing it?

ii.

"many young people believe
the independence
fostered by a career
is necessary,
not only for their own self-esteem,
but as a foundation
for a future partnership."
—The New York Times Magazine, *April 1987*

Let's clear aside some economic business, because it has to be stated but it only has to be stated once. In *Madame Bovary* (misremembered as a romantic novel, one of the ultimate ro-mantic novels: Remember that in fact Emma eats arsenic be-cause her credit line has been shut off and she can't afford to pay it back on), Flaubert gets off a breath-taker of a line about the connection between dollars and love. "Of all the icy winds that blow on love, a request for money is the most chilling and havoc-wreaking." When money problems obtrude, they tend to push everything else aside. The age for first marriage had been dropping steadily throughout the first third of this century. And then—boom! The depression, and suddenly, for three or four years, people stopped marrying. They were afraid to—economic uncertainty bleeds directly into romantic uncertainty. Economic uncertainty lacks sex appeal. We reach out to touch another, and our arms are propped up by money, by confidence in our jobs. Otherwise, we bring them only problems, only problems we can't solve ourselves. We don't want to bring problems to another person. We want to bring solutions. Victor Lindquist told us that the self-worth that comes from a job is incalculable, but it isn't. It *is* calculable. In the 1930s, you had no jobs, and you had a tremendous, calculable slowdown in the number of marriages. In the nineties, we've had a similar slowdown.

The average age for first marriage went up every year in the eighties. Every year. On the other hand, in the fifties, when there were jobs and money around for everyone, the average age for first marriage dropped every year. (It landed at around twenty-one. Separate early-sixties marrying ages by sex, and you get 22.6 for men, 20.3 for women.) Those predictions about large families and all the rest, from the late seventies, were based on the notion that the jobs would be there for the asking. When that fantasy cleared up, the marrying age started to climb. By the middle eighties, the age for first marriage was already the highest in the century: 25.5 for men, 23.3 for women. And the number of people—this is from the census—moving *out* of their mid-twenties without having married was already 40 percent higher than it had been in 1970.

# Late Bloomers

So it went until now. So many of us have had the sense that marriages were coming later. In our surveys, when we asked people what surprises their mid-twenties had arranged for them, many reported surprise at still being unmarried. They had expected to be espoused to somebody. When our parents asked us why we weren't married, or if we were planning to marry soon, we would tell them that no one we knew was getting married, really. But you can't be sure without the numbers. Here they are. By 1987, there were half as many married couples in their mid-twenties as in the sixties—the time when our own parents were mid-twenties young marrieds. (In 1987, only 16 percent of young men and 32 percent of young women were married—in 1960, however, 32 percent of the men and 51 percent of the women had married, had made that little jump.) For those of us in the twenty-five- to thirty-year-old bracket, the differences were even larger. In 1970, only 19 percent of all men and 10 percent of all women in that age group had never married. Twenty years later, those census numbers more than doubled: 47 percent of all such men had never married, along with 30 percent of all women. The spring 1993 census showed that the marrying age had increased again: It was now 24.4 for women and 26.5 for men. This was the latest age for first marriage since the census began recording numbers, in 1890. (Another survey, by a demographer out of Minnesota, put the ages even higher: 27 for women, 29 for men.) So when we had the notion that people were marrying later, we were right—you can usually trust a guess like that. People really *were* marrying later. Why?

The newspaper and magazine people, and the census people, put the blame on the economy—they fell into the Fuchs camp. When there aren't jobs, there aren't betrothals. A young woman named Julia Carlisle wrote in *The New York*

*Times* about her experiences being young and unemployed; these conditions did not prove a dependable aphrodisiac. "Love, well, there is love. We have loved and lost. We may even have loved and won. But there is little time for love—the kind that comes with the cherry blossoms—when you're unemployed. Love is a simple lifeline, a desperate clinging to a shoulder as we tabulate taxes we cannot pay. The rent, the car payments and the credit card bill are all figured under the glare of a light bulb, in tears and shouting, in rushes of frustration at the only thing we have, the one we 'love.' "

When you're inviting a date over, you clean the house. That's pretty standard. You clean yourself, and then you clean your house. You wash the sheets (if you're feeling lucky), you try to fold the bathroom towels the way you've seen people do it in guest baths, you make what you can of the kitchen floor and tub. Because what you want to offer is yourself at your best. You want to say: Join my life, it's clean and nice in here. But you can hardly go on such dates when you haven't got a job. You can hardly bear on such dates if the inevitable question—and what do *you* do—is likely to be painful, is likely to make you wince. It's going to be a two-part answer: "Well, I *really* want to, but right now I'm . . ." No, you aren't likely to want to invite people to step into that messy room, accounted for with an embarrassed smile. So you stop dating, or you stop dating "seriously"—you look for people below your old ambition level, people who won't be offended by your ladder-spot in life. And then you can hardly love them, the way you used to love people when you had a more likely fantasy you. You're still trying to provide the old fantasy you with the right mate. You hardly want to let that fantasy down. So you date without the prospect of marriage. Your dates become dead-end, become McJobs—they're loves without the possibility of advancement, loves where you'll be in the same position, if you choose to stay, for years and years.

When Lindquist and people like him said that the economy for people our age was the worst it's been since the depression, they were giving us a hint. When economics writer Robert Kuttner wrote that the country was experiencing "a remarkable generational economic distress, a depression of the young," he was saying the same thing. We've gone back to that Depression era with jobs, and we've gone back with romance, too. Young people were unwilling to marry then—their lives weren't certain, their lives hadn't relaxed into routine—and they're unwilling to marry now. The jobs didn't come, so the marriages didn't come either. As Flaubert said, no wind blows icier on love than the need for cash.

### iii.
### aids

But we also know it's not that simple, don't we? We know it's not the economy, or not *just* the economy. It's not just AIDS, it's not just the divorces. It's a combination, and it's all part of the same thing.

People will always say—*Time* said this, and then so did *The Washington Post,* and *Newsweek,* and ABC and everyone else—that AIDS ended the sexual revolution, that AIDS changed our sexual habits. But that isn't true. The sexual revolution was ended before AIDS. The longings that brought Reagan into the White House could have told you it had ended, and AIDS didn't begin appearing among gay men until 1981. It didn't begin appearing among heterosexuals until three years later. Men we talked to would sigh, "If I'd been adult in the seventies—man, I would have been *all over the place.*" But it doesn't feel true. Men, somehow, fooled women into adopting their own locker-room ethic in the early seventies. They somehow got women to see it as a logical extension of their own feminist movement. But that trick wasn't likely to last, even without AIDS, without herpes, without chlamydia. Like divorce, and lots of borrowing by the government, and putting college onto the installment plan, the sexual revolution (which basically meant people going to bed with people they didn't know terribly well) was a late-century experiment that had to be tried sooner or later. But it didn't suit anyone.

Women tried wanting what men want; and then they went back to wanting what women want. And what women want from men is fine. It's the same thing they've always wanted—the sex of course, but also the person in the bed, in the airplane seat next to yours, across the tablecloth, riding in your head as you voyage through the day. Not many, just one. A witnessing presence. And the nice thing is, this is what men want, too. We know it is, because it is what everyone seeks out, and what they have always sought out. Men might complain about women, but the complaints seem intended mostly to establish a point about reluctance. You can learn this by spending an evening with a bunch of single men. They will talk about movies, about their jobs, or about their hobbies. But eventually, the conversation will wind itself around to the only point, and all they will talk about is how much they want—someone. For the sex, of course, but for the person in the bed, the woman in the airplane seat next to yours, the fellow passenger on your lifetime's voyage. That's what they want, too. The person who looks at you and says: You turned out okay. You are just the person I want to spend most of my time with. Somehow, we spend all these months and years preparing a personality, piecing it together, testing it out on people, getting feedback from our pals. But the way you hand it in, the way you get it graded, is when another person looks at you and says, You are just right. In all the world, you are the sole person I want to be with. Just you.

AIDS has become a kind of excuse—one method for explaining why our sexual attitudes seem to have regressed from the high-water mark they hit in the seventies. It's our explanation for actually wanting the conventional thing. It's a good excuse: We aren't antimodern—we're afraid of AIDS. AIDS—and herpes first—gave women an out from a mode of behavior many of them never much liked. And AIDS gave men an out from pursuing a kind of male behavior that no longer had relevance for them. Imagine a world without AIDS. How different—beyond the condoms—would our sexual lives be?

We've all had our AIDS panics, of course. But these usually occurred after we left an old lover, or when we met a new one. These happened at times of maximum emotional anxiety, and in a way spared us having to address that anxiety directly. The AIDS idea—that when you go to bed with someone, you're really going to bed with all the people they've been to bed with—it's true *anyway,* even without AIDS. *That's* what's scary. You're the product of all those old loves: Certain emotional muscles have been overdeveloped. Some have gone undeveloped entirely. What will this mean with a new person? Have our previous experiences made it impossible for us to be with the proper person? Have we mentally misoutfitted ourselves, disqualified ourselves, by choices in the past? It's what an intelligent person would fear every time they met a new person.

Or maybe AIDS, like much else, has simply lost its capacity to shock. We were surprised. Now we've incorporated it. After all, we keep being told what an impact it's had on us. In a 1992 article *The New York Times* wryly ran during Valentine's week, the chairman of a college task force on AIDS explained, "There's a great sense of chaos now when young people consider sexual activity. They frequently tell you that the risks they perceive far outweigh the pleasures of sex." In the same article, the young feminist Paula Kamen explained, "People today are much more cautious about making a commitment, perhaps so cautious they just can't sit back and let romance take over. There are too many things that can go wrong and maybe destroy your whole future or kill you." Cut out that last "kill you"—as if Kamen had remembered at the last instant that this was to be an AIDS quote—and you have the worries about romance that people have always had, the intelligent response to love as practiced in the Western world.

When we hit the road and interviewed people for this book, they would talk about AIDS—you could tell they knew they were supposed to; it was one of the things they expected we would want to know—but their discussions of it always went off on weird angles. There was never the "terror" that we had expected to hear about—there was the sense of another bit of info being added to the mix, a mix that was going in that direction anyway. AIDS affects people sideways, by exacerbating concerns that were already there. Adina Albert, an unemployed twenty-five-year-old in Boston, explained of AIDS, "My friends are obsessed. A lot of them are just obsessed. I mean a lot of them are so busy worrying about these things they never even end up *having* sex. I mean it's amazing. I just don't think about it at all. I just figure, for me it's 'Live Free or Die.' I don't think it's going to happen to me. But if it is, I just don't think there's anything I can do about it. I have this strange sense that I'm not going to get it from having sex with somebody. I'm going to get it from the dentist. I worry about *that* all the time. I'm so panicked, I'm sure that if there's a way to get it from thin air, I'm getting it. But I've never worried about getting it from sex."

As she spoke more, she could see how AIDS affected friends of hers. But the effect was largely to agitate emotional considerations. "One couple, they're ridiculous. It's amazing. There was this one guy a friend of mine was dating for a while, and they spent so much time worrying about so many things that they never even got around to having sex. I'm not talking about diseases. I mean, you could just use condoms. I mean they were both just so worked up about these things that they never even had any fun at all. I mean, what's the point of that?"

Jay Boyle, a twenty-eight-year-old Chicago lawyer, was adamant that AIDS *had* changed behaviors. "It's made people warier, more careful, more cautious. I mean, you're going to be cautious anyway, but this makes people hesitant, reluctant." According to Jay, it had made sexual practices more varied, in an unexpected way. "People are nervous about actually having intercourse. So you end up doing other things. It's the whole adolescence thing. Sometimes I find myself doing things I hadn't done since high school. Other times I find myself doing things I *never* thought I'd do. In a strange way, it's made a lot of us a lot more perverse, because the main item is off the menu, but you still have that drive, don't you? You still want to do *something* when you're in bed."

But adults have always known that making the wrong romantic choice can have drastic consequences: that marrying the wrong person at twenty-five can end with a divorce at thirty-five, and a situation that will alter the direction of your entire life. Tensions about the male-female equation tend to express themselves through a specific problem. In *this* era, in our era, we have a wariness toward commitment, toward choosing someone. There's Liz Sherrill's remark to remember. Our parents—those lucky people who married so young in the 1950s and '60s—had sleepwalked into their marriages, into their life choices. What Liz saw since the sixties was something else. She saw a conscious life, of examined choices. That life is simply more trying than sleepwalking. It means you are going to be testing very carefully the person you choose; it means you are going to be wary and cautious and hesitant. And it means you would do those things without AIDS. AIDS is certainly unanticipated. But after our experience of divorce in the seventies, it just seems more of the same thing. Another reason to be cautious. But not the only reason.

iv.
## "setting up your own household is the biggest expense that an average American undertakes—either renting their own apartment or buying a single-family home."
—*Richard Hokenson,* Barron's, *January 1991*

There's a strictly selfish reason you should root for us—if you're an older person, if you're not a parent. If you're a parent, you're rooting for us to marry because you know it's the socioeconomic event Fuchs wrote of, that will mark the end of this limbo. It's the step that will allow us to move on, to stop rehearsing for adult life. You're rooting for us personally. But if you're just a person living in the same economy we are, there's a commonsense reason to want us to find jobs, to want us to have enough money so we can invite other people to be permanent guests in our lives. Married couples account for 55 percent of all the spending in America. And the items bought by people just starting out in marriage account for 20 percent of our GDP. When you get married, you have to buy all kinds of things: You have to buy dishes and beds and televisions and cars and dishwashers and towels—you have to go on a socially sanctioned spending spree. The economy needs that kind of input—it needs it every year. The economic demographer Richard Hokenson—he works for Donaldson, Lufkin, Jennerette—has made this theory his specialty. It's his whole act. According to Hokenson's theory, it's the twenty-five-year-olds who count most. That's the age when people tend to marry and set up their own households. According to Hokenson's research, it's been such twenty-five-year-olds who, with their buying needs, have generally kept the economy from slipping into recession. And, when the country is in recession, it's those marrying twenty-five-year-olds who spend the country back out.

The technical term for buying futons and things is "household formation." Hokenson found that, with the hard first year of the recession affecting us, and with the age for first marriage climbing so high, fewer households were being formed. Predictably, 1990—the year one million of us lost our jobs—had seen the first annual decline in household formation *ever*. Hokenson predicted that, unless there was some shift in the position of young people, there were going to be many fewer households forming in the nineties, which would have predictable effects on the economy. In 1990, the rate of new household formation was going up by only 0.56 percent a year. In the more robust 1980s, the rate had been 1.3 percent, and in the 1970s it had been 2.2 percent. That number, he suggested, showed why the country was having such a hard time getting *out* of recession, and also suggested why we might have slipped into it in the first place.

Hokenson, during a long interview with the financial magazine *Barron's* in December of 1991, saw what he called "the End of Growth" coming, because twenty-five-year-olds could no longer afford to get married. Without the marriages—another cold economic light shined into the comfortable muddle of our romantic lives—the country was never going to work out of its present trough. In the past, Hokenson had found, only about 6 percent of all adults never married. For our generation, Hokenson thought the number of never-marrieds—all those people not attending life's prom, missing most of the experiences that the common run of life has to offer—might go as high as 30 percent. For Hokenson, this was a very scary number. And it's a scary number for us, too. If Fuchs is right, and getting a job and a spouse are the events that end adolescence, then we're likely to remain stuck for quite a while. And if Hokenson is right, the recession will linger, too. It's nice to read that our romantic troubles are of concern to the nation—that marrying, in addition to being for ourselves, will be a little patriotic. But it will be nice when we can afford it.

As *Business Week* (not the most sentimental publication) explained the same year, the whole country would be hurt so long as people our age were left out of the economy; if we could not afford to enroll ourselves, as previous generations had done, into the culture as husbands and wives and fathers and mothers. "Every generation will be hurt if busters put fewer dollars into circulation. If busters enter their thirties and forties with reduced real incomes, they'll buy less, too: fewer houses, cars, and luxury goods of every variety." As the magazine summarized, "That would end what for most

Americans has been fifty years of pretty good times." A young man named Bryan Burket, writing in *The Washington Post,* made a similar appeal, in personal terms. Writing of his own stalled position as an unemployed college graduate, he reminded people older than ourselves that there was a direct correlation between our economic achievement and their own comfort. "I have no panacea for the problems that plague our economy, but I ask that those in authoritative positions remember where they started out. Use the millions of intelligent, skillful men and women who were born after 1963. Consider us, because in the end your own quality of life will depend on us." Our wariness about marriage is our own creation, and the creation of the times we live in. But now that many of us are ready to shuck that wariness—we've learned what we're supposed to look for, we're going to have successful marriages—the problem is humiliatingly out of our hands. We must wait until the money is available to us— and it is reassuring to read that if the money is never available to us, it will soon be available to no one.

### v.

"people didn't get married because they had found someone. it wasn't a treasure hunt. marriage was more like musical chairs. wherever you were when the music of being single stopped, that's where you sat."
—*Lorrie Moore,* Anagrams: A Novel, *1986*

So here we are. Mostly unmarried. Mostly waiting to get married. Mostly unable to afford getting married. Journalists criticized us for not starting families at the proper age—they saw it as evidence of immaturity—but in most ways it was the most mature response. We weren't going to stumble into the same error as our folks. And we weren't going to start families (which meant have children) until we could afford to support them. Under the circumstances, anything else would have been *immature*. Under the circumstances, America should look at our experiences over the last two decades and congratulate itself for having raised such a levelheaded generation. For a dopier generation would have gone ahead and had kids anyway. And then real trouble would have begun.

What have we lost? For one, it was a pleasure having young parents. Divorced or not, it was a pleasure, when your school had open house, to have these young people showing up, these charming people who still had energy. Whatever happens now, of course, we aren't going to be able to give that to our own children. Whatever our preferences would have been, we'll be late parents, the latest ever. When you choose to have children, you are setting the schedule for the next twenty years. When we choose to have children *now,* we'll be penciling in appointments into our fifties—we won't be out of it in our forties, the way our parents were. We've cost our kids that nice experience of having young parents, and we've cost ourselves that nice experience of being still young when our children are out of the house.

And then there's all the dating—so much that *another* new term had to be invented for the way we do it, the way we do it now: "serial monogamy." It's the combination of the long trial period—during which our lovers eliminate themselves as husbands and wives—and the desire to find someone who's healthy and more or less stand by them. We've engaged in all these trial marriages. A year with one person.

Two years with another. Nine months with someone else. Many of our parents have one divorced spouse—and if they're lucky, if they're on good terms with them, they can call that ex-husband or wife up and chat things over. This is a person who knows you well. This is, in a weird, late-twentieth-century way, a member of your extended family. But most of us have three or four ex-husbands and wives. We have any number of ex-loves who know us well, whom we can call and swap notes with. We've been prepping for marriage. But we've also been prepping for divorce, learning how to divide joint property, how to argue over owed money, how to close off your old love-response toward someone who you, officially anyway, no longer love.

And we envy the people who do get married. There's a predictable sequence—and this of course is not if they're very rich; for a while, in our mid-twenties, we were attending weddings, and then we noticed that most of the marriages were of the rich kids we'd known at school—in which you get a job and become ready. Finally, you get the job you need to pay off your loan, to begin living in the middle class. Then you turn around and begin looking for someone to marry. Finally. The writer Lorrie Moore—who has an acid pen—compared marriage to the game musical chairs. The person you marry, she wrote, is the person you're sitting next to when the "music of being single" stops. We've seen it, haven't we? All the sacrifices you've made, the things you've turned your back on. The minute you're established, you start grabbing for those things again.

Michael Allen, a twenty-eight-year-old copywriter in Ohio, describes his own marriage. He got his job—and then he was simply ready to marry. "I hadn't dated Lynn at all before we got married. We were buddies at school. She was dating someone else, I was dating someone else. Lynn was dating a rugby player, and I was dating a girl freshman. We always commented on each other's choice of mates. She moved to London. I moved to Birmingham and got my job. She was going to come back to the States. I said come visit me. And she never left. We had separate apartments for a year, and then we were married."

Just like that: Their lives settle into predictability, with money, and then they are married. We look on the married among us with a certain kind of wonder, a certain kind of envy. They have been relieved of a great homework assignment. The people who marry, they are like the ones who get their term papers in early, the ones who finish an exam in record time. You can see the tension, the pressure, has gone out of their faces. They've gotten this little assignment that life gives—find a mate, get on with it—off their backs. And we're still in there trying to get the thing completed.

We will make better choices than our parents made, because we'll have tried this out longer and will know what to look for. That's the good news. The bad news, though, is that by twenty-six, twenty-seven, we already *know* what we're looking for. Now the fear is that we'll meet the right person too early, before we're able to afford a marriage. That our emotional connection will be deformed by the pressures Julia Carlisle wrote about, that we won't have the cash handy to take the relationship to its next step, and so relationships that would have flourished will wither. This is the risk we run; and until we have the money, we'll stay in the serial monogamy game, the musical chairs game. We'll wait until we have the money, so we can walk up to the musicians and pay them to make the music stop.

# vi.
## in situ parentis

"My current job is low-paying, no benefits at all, no sick pay, little vacation. One tenth of my salary is gone to student loans. It has been very rough to take a job after school and not be able to afford things I could while I was in college and graduate school. Why leave school to a lower standard of living?"

—Gary R. Reinhardt,
Richmond, Virginia, twenty-seven

i.

## "havens in a slow economy"

—Los Angeles Times, *July 1991*

You could look at this info—at these surprises—and if you had a clear eye, you could say it probably hadn't worked out. No, it hadn't worked out that great for us. As kids we were programmed to mature extremely quickly. And then we'd found—just at the age when we could have put those lessons into practice—that we couldn't get any older. We could get to a certain point, become what priests and rabbis call "young people," and then couldn't become grown-ups. We owed huge amounts of money to big financial institutions when we came out of college, but we couldn't find jobs. We were ready to select our mates but couldn't close the deal. We were and still are citizens of a country in which we can't quite afford to become actual adults.

How did we deal with it? There were two draft deferments from life. Graduate school was one, of course. Graduate school, as Sonja Trojica told us, was "the perfect hideout." Another woman, Sarah Cherkis, told us of a dream she had, in which she and her boyfriend had somehow wound up at graduate school. Everyone she knew was there. They were all graduate students. In the dream, graduate school was bliss; in the dream, it was paradise for young people. "I had an image of us, of me going to graduate school and him coming with me. And there was no embarrassment at all. I felt relieved and happy. Totally. And I met people. It was funny, because I was with other women in the graduate program. And they were wives of graduate students, and they were all living off the graduate stipend. You can live poorly in graduate school, but you're not down and out. You can *live.* There's no cultural bias against you. None at all. And these women had children. I was really like, Wow, these people can start their families and everything and be graduate students. I felt happy to be back in that environment." Why? "When you're a student, there's always a *becoming* of something. You're not there yet, but you're becoming. And you're being taken care of by something. A bigger sort of thing. You're given your medical insurance. They give you this measly medical insurance, but you have it. They give you a better deal than corporations do now. People who have loans—and a lot of people in our generation, a lot of us have loans—your loans *stop.* I have deferred my loans as much as I could defer them since I've been out of college."

The advantage of graduate school, as Sarah saw it, is simple. You can live poor, but with your head high. You lapse back into potential mode. Living on $6,000 a year in the real world is an embarrassment; it's a failure in front of your family and friends. Living on $6,000 a year in graduate school is honorable. Everyone sees you as a prospect again. During the early-eighties recession, people our age had hidden out in graduate school—applications for the 1983 graduate school

academic season went up by 20 percent. The numbers sub-
sided when the economy heated up. But after 1989, graduate
school applications went through four straight years of increased applications. The Law School Admissions Council
reported a record-high 95,000 students applying to law
school (unfortunately, as the *Chicago Tribune* would report in
1992, half of graduating law students were failing to find
jobs). The number of college students intending to pursue
advanced degrees jumped up to 60 percent—from 25 percent at the end of the seventies. From 1989 to 1993, the
number of students taking the Graduate Record Exam—the
grad school SAT—ballooned from 300,000 to 411,000 a
year. In 1993, medical schools had their best year ever for
applications. As one doctor asked *The Boston Globe*, "How
many unemployed physicians do you know?"

Those students who had academic credentials and
could bear the additional debt—the average graduate
school debt is around $30,000—were bowing out honor-
ably from the economy, keeping their heads down until
things cleared up. They were returning to a student lifestyle that was in some measure gratifying. The other solution was leaving the country. By 1993, *The New York Times*
was reporting there were forty thousand young Americans
living in Prague, where the living was still pretty cheap.
There were similar numbers in Japan, in Europe. We were
looking around, getting the lay of the land, and deciding to
beat it. *New York* magazine ran a long story in 1993 on the
many young Americans living in Moscow. The expatriates
living in Czechoslavakia told one newspaper, "Everyone's
overqualified for what they can get in the States." In
Prague, on the other hand, they found jobs as journalists,
as lawyers, as businesspeople, in an environment where
rents were still fairly cheap, where restaurants were still

fairly cheap. Where you could imitate American middle-class living, with the sole disadvantage being that you were no longer in America. One twenty-four-year-old woman expressed her feelings to *The Boston Globe* in a very sad way: "Someone described it to me," she said, "as an extension of college." It was as if she could remember only one time in which she was treated as a skilled and valuable adult.

Others who had no money made a third deferment choice, the most painful one. They bit the bullet and moved back to their parents' homes. For a generation that was raised to be adults in their teens, being teens as adults was the final irony, and an extraordinary surprise.

ii.

## "today's young adults—if they spread their wings at all—are flying back home in flocks."

—Los Angeles Times, *April 1986*

Moving home is deadly. Moving home is the killer. Moving home is an admission—whatever it took to make it outside, man, I didn't have it. You'd better raise me again. You and me—you say to your parents—we worked up a prototype model of your child. You worked on it pretty in-depth for eighteen years. And now I've been working on it solo for five years. Or seven years. And you know what? It doesn't work. We wanted to collaborate on a model that would function out there under road test conditions. Now, I'm back for some retooling.

"Boomeranging"—the practice got it's name from a 1987 article in *American Demographics*—was the activity that set everyone off. This was the great change that came a few months before the *Time* article in 1990. The census reported that three quarters of all young men under the age of twenty-five were back in their parents' houses, waiting it out again. And this was such a surprise for everyone that they had to find a way to account for it. Observers said we were trying to hide out from adulthood. After all, young people for fifty years had pretty well managed to get out and stay out of their parents' homes. Even through the golden era of parenting, even from those luxury, appliance-ridden paradises of the fifties and sixties. American kids got out of their parents' houses and stayed out. Now they were coming back, and until everyone started accepting what had happened in the economy (the "generational depression" Kuttner was talking about), they had no idea how to account for it.

We interviewed Ken Rubiner the night before he moved back to his parents'. Was he moving back because he loved his folks, especially? Nope. Was he moving back because he found the adult world too daunting? Nope. Ken is a lawyer—this book has been full of lawyers; it was the hedge so many liberal arts majors tried out, before the bottom fell out of lawyering and everyone had to look for a new hedge—and he has kept his job. Why is he going back? "There's no reason at all but financial difficulties that I'm in. When you're living in New York, with this type of rent, you're right on the edge. What I mean is that you never quite make it. You always come up a little bit short and end up eating tuna for three or four days in a row, or whatever it is you need to do to get by." His girlfriend, he foresaw, was going to be a problem; she lived in the city, and Ken's parents lived in the suburbs. "It's a big adjustment. But I'll have some money, and maybe I'll have a better social life because I'll be able to afford it." We'd read so much about the emotional reasons for moving home—before they came up with the Austrailianism for it, people who moved home were called "cling kids" or, most brutally, "failed adults"—that we wanted to verify with Ken why he was moving back. "It's completely financial. My job is here. My girlfriend is here. But I decided something had to change, something had to give. If I didn't make a move this way, to my parents', I'd either have to pick up a second job or I was never going to get out of this hole and never reach the point of financial security that I wanted to reach. So it's a long-term-type move—meaning I'm doing this for the purpose of the long-term goal, which is being independent." Ken said he felt like the one thing no American ever wants to feel like—he applied to himself the term Americans most fear. So we let him in on how many other people had had to move home in the last few years. Ken grinned and used the verboten word again. "That's great," he said. "I didn't know that. Now I don't feel like such a loser."

According to the 1960 census, just under 10 percent of all young adults over twenty-five were continuing to live with their parents. Forty percent of those under twenty-five were also at home. It was something you did—according to the ethos of the time—until you got married. By the time of the 1993 census, those numbers had gone haywire. In 1990, as we've said, *American Demographics* and *Time* reported that a full three quarters of young men under twenty-five were still living at home, and this was the doomsday number. This was the number that traveled all over the media, popping up in a newspaper column, then fluttering off to be uttered on television, then diving back into another magazine. (For some reason no one has figured out, women our age are somewhat less likely to end up back home. A sociologist named Allan Schnaiberg theorized that marrying younger gets them out of the boomeranging pool, gets them off the hook.) In the 1993 census, 58 percent of all young people under twenty-five had returned. The majority. Between the ages of twenty-five and thirty, one out of three of us were living with their folks. Over thirty, one out of four. As of 1993, eighteen million people in our general age category had the same address they'd had in high school, in junior high. The advance over the 1960 numbers goes without saying. There weren't the jobs, and there wasn't the money, and so there wasn't the independence.

Susan Littwin's book *The Postponed Generation* in 1986 set the tone for the articles that would come after it. It was a carnival tone in which some softness on the part of kids—the dreaded American quality of softness—was responsible for their running out of options. The information that large groups of us were moving back home was repeated all over the place like a kind of fascinating dirty joke. The article titles from the period tell you everything. "Today's Graduates May Be Too Young at Heart," "Young Beyond Their Years," "The Younger Generation that Never Grew Up," "More Young Single Men Hold On to Apron Strings," "The Clinging Kid," "Comeback Kids," "Finding the Way to Go Home," "You Can Go Home Again," "Grown Children Show You Can Go Home Again," "Grow Up, Twenty-Somethings, You Can Go Home Again," "Just Call 'Em Homeboys," "Just Tell Us When They're Moving Out," "Guess Who's Staying for Dinner?" "What's for Dinner, Mom?" "Still Footing the Bills," "Back in the Fold," "Back to the Nest," "Nest-Dwellers," "Young Adults Crowd Empty Nest," "Young Adults Return to Nest."

In the early nineties came a new tone. A kind of warming toward these "failed adults" occurred. Academics were studying the trend and they concluded the economy, above all, was the determining factor in sending us back to our parents. Schnaiberg, a professor at Northwestern, had been studying boomerang kids since the middle eighties. When asked why boomeranging had increased, he gave a simple answer. "If you graduated from college in the sixties and seventies, you did not have to be all that diligent to survive, get a decent job, get married, and stumble into life. These days it is much tougher. Housing costs have risen dramatically. And white-collar employment is shrinking, even as the number of college graduates continues to rise each year. A diploma no longer offers you much hope of gaining access to the executive washroom, unless you are there to clean it. Given the current state of the economy, parents may have to choose between having independent young adults and having middle-class young adults."

When *The New York Times* explored this position, you could tell it had become the new norm. In the mid-eighties, the *Times* had taken a pretty strong stance against parentally dependent adults. In May of 1993, there was a more understanding tone. New hard facts about people our age had now to be digested. One psychologist quoted in the piece suggested to parents, "You have to ask yourself what it means to you personally that your child is a disappointment. Does it mean that you're a failure? Does it mean that what you've accomplished won't be passed on to the next generation?" The newspaper itself had some advice for parents of such disappointing children. "Look for ways in which your children have met your aspirations for them. These may not be obvious."

Returning to our parents' homes was another sad fact about our generation. The last sad fact. The punch line.

## iii.

# "he's in the backyard,
# raking leaves."

*—The mother of a twenty-six-year-old boomerang
kid (who asked that we not use her name),
January 1993*

When you pressed parents further, however, you found just
how thin the reassurance spread by this last wave of articles
was. Said one Philadelphia mother after telling us that her
son was cleaning the yard, "We're all looking forward to the
time when he'll be able to move out and be self-supporting."
This mother, who owned two homes—"Many children of my
friends don't expect to be able to ever own their own
home"—discussed what she missed by having her son return
to her household. "I'd certainly like to have my privacy. You
know, a little more. It's just *nicer,* at this point in life. We've
already had all those years of raising little kids, and pets, and
intrusions, and responsibilities. And I think it would be nicer
not to have to worry if someone comes home late, or if
they're coming home at all. Just to have to answer for yourself and your husband. I look forward to that day. I feel that's
the way it should be. Adults on their own. Making their own
way."

And for people our age, the reassurances didn't hold, either. They spoke of "surrendering" by moving back home.
Of the loss of their self-esteem. Some tried to put the best
face on it—speaking of the chance to "better know their parents"—but there's a limit to how much you can accomplish
this way. You can adjust *yourself,* your own reaction to a situation, but the world's reaction doesn't change. It's embar-

rassing to have to check back in to your parents' home. "I hated saying it," one woman told us. "At any family function, it was just lie-o-rama, whenever anyone asked where I was living or what I was doing." One guy told us about the difficulties in dating. "I would meet somebody, and I had to immediately decide right away whether I was comfortable letting them know I lived at home. And with people I didn't know very well, the answer was usually 'no.' Period." A woman spoke of tiptoeing up the stairs when she came home late at night—and of being struck by how much like high school the situation was. "Then I thought—wait a second. I'm not in high school anymore. That really hit me then."

Sonja and Robert, who had taught in Lyons, have been living with Rob's parents outside Boston for nine months. "Nine months," Sonja says. "The horror of it." She speaks feelingly of the haze of living in a parent's house, the danger of slipping back into childhood patterns, of letting parents take care of everything.

"I've known other people who have gone home for a certain period. For financial reasons. Rob's cousin. He had just gotten married, and he and his wife had moved home. They had both tried to get jobs in Houston, and they were home for a few months. They weren't happy. Actually, it's funny because as far as I was concerned, I kind of looked down on them. I was thinking, I can't believe Jim and Elaine are living at home. I said to myself, Oh my god, they're married and at home, can you believe that? I thought it was immature—and demeaning, sort of. Because they had to go back to Mom and Dad. It's a huge blow to your psyche. It's sort of like a failure; the failure is to go home. And now I know that other people are saying, God, Sonja and Robert are living at home, can you believe it?

"Now, four years later, I know a lot of people who have

chosen to live with their parents. Friends of mine from high school and college. It's kind of crazy. We've all done it for four or five months. You do it while you're looking for work, waiting for that jump-start to happen.

"There's certainly a money advantage. We save at least seven hundred dollars a month. Boston rent is really high. I mean, we couldn't even live in this area, to be honest, it's so expensive. If we stay another six months we'll have saved two or three thousand dollars. We're not paying rent anymore. That's over. We've saved all that money on rent, so that's nice.

"On the other hand, I basically have less freedom because I don't have my own space, I don't have my own vehicle, I don't have my own whatever. It's a completely temporary thing, I know. But it can be very frustrating while you're in it. It's not your own home. I'm constantly feeling like a guest. I tend to be less sort of forceful of my desires. I tend to tread very softly.

"I sleep in a separate bedroom. I don't necessarily like it. I miss Robert at night, but it's not a big deal. Sexual issues are complexified, they totally are. We've just sort of put everything on hold. Or you sneak around. It's the kind of thing you used to do when you were in high school. It's kind of demeaning, in a way, sneaking around. It's totally like that; it's this funny thing. It's gotten to the point where I'm getting that feeling of displacement. I'm not doing my work. I'm wasting time.

"And this makes it harder to get back on the adult track. That's the twist. The best way to get out of their house is to keep sending out more résumés. But it's harder than in your own house. Rob gets up at eleven-thirty, reads the paper, drinks his coffee. We watch much more TV here than we ever did in our whole lives. We never watched TV. I don't know why, but it's just like this place where you can go very easily and just zone out. It's almost like you're in a sleep state. It takes very little energy.

"Six months from now I'd rather be somewhere else. Only because I need my own space. I want to have my own space. When we have the same setup in America we had in Lyons I'll feel like an adult again. I probably will, when I get that setup. Until I do, I probably won't."

And there is the irony. As she spoke, Sonja kept smiling in soft disbelief at her own sentences, as if she couldn't quite believe that this story was coming out of her mouth. Sonja had been a child of divorce. She had helped take care of her younger sister, she had worked very hard to put herself through college, she had gone away to Europe when she couldn't find work in America, and had even convinced her boyfriend to go along with her. And she had become, after an upbringing that had required that she take care of herself from a very young age, someone else's guest. That was her achievement. She had gotten to be an adult for a while; now she was waiting to be adult again. She would laugh, as if she could see the ironies she was stumbling over, and yet couldn't keep herself from stumbling. To have worked that hard, that long, and to end up not in her own home, with her own family, but in someone else's home, in someone else's family, was a situation that her education trained her to accept only as comedy. A comedy whose star she was, and with whose dialogue she was comfortable, but whose setting and action she felt powerless to change.

And this really was the last surprise for the generation. The being raised so quickly—that wasn't so bad, and for a while there had been the pleasure of being the wisest kids ever, the least naïve kids ever. And taking out loans for college—there had been something swanky in that, too, in lying

on financial forms the same way our parents lied on tax returns, learning to do that little adversarial dance with the
government. But these things had been about maturing
*quickly*. The pleasure in the trade-off was that with each
thing we gave up (being children who were separated from
adult responsibilities, being students who were paid for by
their parents), we were moving closer to being grown-up
ourselves. The early "R" movies, the early drinking, the early
sex—it was our point that there should be no adult experiences we were excluded from, no information we should be
protected from.

We came out of college into this dismal job picture. We
came out of college owing huge amounts of money. Living at
home is the punch line to all that. To grow up so fast, to
support ourselves—and then to have to return to our parents' house, to start the cycle again. It was a terminal surprise, the final surprise. After the various adaptations we
made, to learn that we couldn't quite swing it, that our parents' homes were going to contract to take us in. At the end
of all our changes, this last change in how Americans disen-
tagled themselves from their families, for the influence and
protection of their parents. You started once before. Now
you must start again.

# vii.
# conclusion

When you hang around people your own age, you begin to wonder. You wonder, for example, if gallows humor is dangerous. On some level, after all, the brain is a little captive you carry, a little round being locked in a round shell. It's wholly dependent for its information on five spies—who bring it information on what the outside world sounds, tastes, smells, looks, and feels like. It's independent of us, of the self that acts fairly quickly, that buys a Snickers bar instead of a Reese's, that hops on the local instead of waiting for the express. And there's the danger, in gallows humor, that the brain will overhear it and think it's serious. It will hear us joking with our friends about our fears about health insurance, our sense that we may never get ahead, our suspicion that we may in fact never marry. And our brains will believe it. And then we will believe it, too. We believe what we hear, even if we ourselves are the ones saying it. But then, gallows humor is our meeting place.

There can't be that much question—not anymore, not in 1994—as to whether there is as much "opportunity" for our generation as there has been in the past. There isn't. At a certain point you're allowed to gather up the evidence, reach a conclusion, and remove the issue from debate. What you begin to wonder is what it does to you, what this time we've had is going to mean later on. Let's assume for the moment that things will open up for us. A common paradoxical observation about people our age: We all believe things are terrible on the whole, but each suspects that we personally will be exempt. Well, let's assume, for the sake of argument, that we're all exempt. That sometime in our late twenties or early thirties, the world will open up for us in a wonderful way. The stall will be over. The gate will be lifted, and we'll return to the swanky vision of ourselves we had before college, before high school. We'll prance out full of fire and jazz and raise a cloud of dust. We'll move back from irony to optimism. We'll drop the position we've occupied for so many years—*clank!* it will say as it hits the dirt behind us.

Or will we? Stephen Gleick, the fellow who attended the Christmas party in the early nineties, says that one thing, after that party, bothered him. The people there—those rich people, who had gotten jobs in television through friends of their parents, who traveled and dressed in style—had looked *younger* to him than he did. Not so much in an absence of wrinkles or gray hairs. Their faces looked unblemished by disappointment. Their heads were held high. They looked like a yachting team that had never lost. Stephen had the notion that his own face, the posture of his own head, told something quite different about him, to anyone who wanted to look. What he wondered was whether—if he positioned himself back on the normal adulthood track—he could ever have their look. He was curious for a sharp and specific professional reason; he thought the people most likely to hire him wanted to see that blemishlessness.

Emerson has a good remark about adversity. In small measures, it can be inoculating. In large measures, it can be crushing. Get enough doors closed in your face and eventually you have a kind of bruise there, in front of your eyes. This was Stephen's fear, and of course, there isn't an answer for it. There isn't even an answer as to whether he'll get to that point, where the question of whether the difficulty of these years shows will matter. If we're still in the difficulty, of course it will show. And by then we'll have made whatever final mental accommodations are necessary, so that we'll believe we never really wanted to join the culture in the first place.

We've done our time this way. We've done this. If we're in our late twenties, we've spent more time now in this phase of our lives than in any other. We've all spent time in relationships we shouldn't have because our boyfriend or girlfriend had a car, was paying the rent: What will that mean to us, what will that kind of memory do to us, five years from now, or ten? We've all learned that employers aren't as automatically interested in us as our teachers were, as our parents were. We've learned that, on some level, we are *without value* to them. It's more information for that little captive up there, riding in our skulls, to sort out. And we can only keep an eye on him so long. Eventually, our attention is distracted by a telephone call, by a television show, by a trip to the movies or the grocery store, and our brains start arranging and classifying the information as they will. And then our brains give that reprocessed stuff back to us as self-image; as daily mood; as daily conversation.

We've seen our older brothers and sisters, a little ahead of us, just a little, having doors closed in their faces for even longer than we have. We see what it's doing to them. We wonder, and we worry, and we want to put our hands to their shoulders and say, Jesus, don't take this too seriously. I remember you from when you were ten, and you were not this way. So don't become some other way now. But we have in this country that great prohibition against asking someone to admit a disappointment. So we will not. We hope they are sanguine about it. We hope we will get out of this before they do.

And we've seen our younger brothers and sisters, a little behind us, never having seen that those doors were open, and in a way that's even worse. For them, it's always been a country of scarcity—they've never developed ambitions to abandon. They've turned away, and we want to take them aside and explain, Look, you know, it seems like we're having the same experience, but I did have the impression, when I was your age, that nice things were going to happen. But this would require admitting disappointments of our own, and we don't want to risk that either. So we say nothing, on either side. And we joke to our peers about our jobs, or our romances, and our brains insatiably gobble up more information that we probably wouldn't like them to have.

It isn't anybody's fault, of course, and we are going to be champion adults when the time does come. Maybe we'll enjoy those things, those light, nice things, more than other generations did, because they will not be automatic to us.

Our own apartments, our own stereos, our own houses, our own jobs: These will have a capacity to delight that one would think had been lost. How wonderful it will be, to stand on our own grass, finally, to look from outside into our own windows, and see the reflection of our own faces, the face that was waiting for us to join it. There it is. From now on, that face will be our face.

And certainly having money was not unalloyed joy for our parents. We know this because of the divorces. We know the way they chose to live was not terrific, because in midstream so many of them decided to reverse that choice. We know that they spent the second parts of their lives making up for the first part. So the moving ahead while young may not have been a great thing. It may have been fine that we missed it. We may be better for it after all.

And this is a cheery thought—and since we like to think in terms of stories and morals, maybe *this* is the good to come out of this extended pause, this endless adolescence. We're optimists, here in the States, and this is the optimistic read. But really, we'd like to say to whoever is stage managing this, you know, we learned that lesson about two or three years ago. That thought perked us up once in the middle of a pretty long night. So how much longer will we have to keep *re*learning it? We get the picture. But it's getting old. You don't have to keep saying it again and again.


The problem of "youth," of the young, becomes paramount when a country is going through a change. And this country is going through a change. It will be slow. But the America of ten years from now—by which time we'll know if we left adolescence or not—is likely to look very different from the America of today, of the mid-1990s. The kids without col-

171

lege degrees are going to be squeezed out. The GDP figures are going to keep crushing them into the ground until they're gone. A lot of the jobs that will remain will have to do with television. And when that happens, all that early training of ours will really come into play. Our economy moved from the organic to the industrial and now it's moving on to the ethereal, to the ephemeral. In the optimistic scenario—one phrase no one our age trusts—America will generate the computerized and televised whims of the world. That's where money will come from in the next century: the manufacture and control of moods. That's something we're good at, too.

In the 1850s, when England's economy was moving from the organic to the industrial, the problem of the young was also debated. Dickens built a whole novel around it— *Bleak House*. The metaphor in the book was a mammoth, convoluted inheritance case. What Dickens was wondering, of course, was what sort of young person was going to inherit his country. He posited two types of young personalities.

The first, Bartholomew Smallweed, is flourishing in the new London. He is fifteen, but is a child who has never been a child; he is an indestructible economic type. The Smallweed family has encouraged its offspring to forsake childhood entirely. They have a "practical character that has discarded all amusements, discounted all story-books, fairy tales, fictions and fables, and banished all levity whatsoever." Thus, according to Dickens, "the gratifying fact" that there have *never* been any children in the Smallweed family, and "the complete men and women whom it has produced have been observed to resemble old monkeys with something depressing on their minds." Bartholomew Smallweed is instead solely concerned with making money. In Dickens's eye, this young person without youth is a human weed, and not even a grand one.

The other new character, Richard Carstone, is a young guy in his early twenties. He *might* be a beneficiary of the endless inheritance case being settled throughout the book. But the sense that some good thing might be coming his way in the future overwhelms Richard. It incapacitates him. He lives in a perpetual suspension, never able to settle down to a profession or commit himself to one present thing. "Everything postponed to that imaginary time!" writes Dickens. "Everything held in confusion and indecision until then!" By the end of the novel, Richard has run through every conceivable occupation but is still mainly waiting for his future to start. By the end of the novel, he has been literally disfigured by deferred hopes. His cousin looks at him and sees "how worn and haggard he looked, even in the fullness of his youth. His hopefulness had long been more painful to me than his despondency. It was so unlike *true* hopefulness, had something so fierce in its determination to *be* hopefulness, that it had long touched me to the heart. It was indelibly in his face. I say indelible, for had the case been forever terminated, according to his brightest visions, the traces of the premature anxiety, self-reproach, and disappointment it had occasioned in him would have remained on his features to the hour of his death."

In the face of a harried London, Dickens saw two responses on the part of youth. Neither was a success. The first was to squeeze out every human thing but ambition and try to make money—to do this was to become nonhuman. The other was to wait motionless for things to turn around, to live on expectations and not on activity—and to do this was to become nonalive. Those seem very like the options we've had, in our time of change. (And Stephen would not like the answer Dickens here gives to his question, of whether delayed hopes would show on your face. Of course they would. And he would certainly not have been cheered by Richard's eventual death by madness, by endless hope.)

Those were Dickens's anxieties about what might happen to the character of youth in the 1850s. Those have been the anxieties people have had about us, in the 1980s and '90s. Would we be Carstones, or would we be Smallweeds? Those who have watched us, who make their living by making guesses about the future, have alternated between one and the other. But the best fate is to be neither. The best fate is to avoid them both.

To wait but to be active; to be active but not to close off, in our pursuit of a settled life, every good thing *about* life. That is the choice we have. History—the particular moment at which we've made our appearance—has given us a complex set of options, and will no doubt continue to frustrate and delight us. As a group, we are old at being young. As a portion of the economy, we are integral to the future of the country, and we hope our elders can remember how much the future quality of their own lives depends, as Hokenson would say, on the present quality of ours.

Our lives, our adult lives, wait ahead of us. But to wait sulkily—this is what is meant by whining, we suppose—is not an option. We must step ahead, as we can. We should remember how we were raised, what our own history has been like, so that when others tell us that our situation is our own fault, we can say, Well, no. We can ask how they would have lived, put through our time. And we can remember, though not inflexibly, the things we used to want, the sort of life we once wished to have. We asked everyone we talked to to define adulthood: Our elders would winsomely laugh, and say they weren't sure they were adults yet, then catch their breath through their smiles to see if we'd been charmed by that. Our friends, our peers, had a number of ideas. Being adult meant being financially independent; being adult meant having children; being adult meant committing to another in life. And throughout the last decade and a half, the culture has tried to suggest ways to be adult: first by scrambling dedicatedly ahead; then by sensibly waiting; then by moving to repair the country. These have been the suggestions to us. But to take another's suggestion of what we should be is not to become ourselves in maturity, but to become something else. It is to become, in a sense, a Smallweed. To sacrifice what we know of our own personalities and to adopt another. We must remember the things we wanted. Adolescence is all about deciding what you want, whittling down those choices to the one that best fits in your hand, the one that most suits the personal shape of your palm. The next step is getting those things; the ability to recognize and acquire the things you want must finally be what is meant by the word *adult*.

# notes

## a meditation

Page 6   " 'Unlucky-looking people' ": Robert Stone, *Dog Soldiers* (New York: Knopf, 1974), p. 18.

Page 7   " 'I worry about money' ": Martin Amis, *Success* (London: Jonathan Cape, 1978), p. 182.

Page 9   **"The Lovely Troubled Daughters"**: John Updike, *Trust Me* (New York: Knopf, 1988), p. 144.

Page 11   " **'I miss the old me'** ": "Poor Prospects: Twentysomethings Find Life Bleak as They Sort Mail, Fret About Their Poverty," *The Wall Street Journal,* July 28, 1993.

Page 11   " **'the generation that never wanted to grow up'** ": "Facing Up to Fortysomething with Marshall Herskovitz," *Sunday Telegraph* (London), October 17, 1993. Herskovitz also observes, "Our generation was so blind we thought being old was a disease other people had that we wouldn't catch. Other generations might have welcomed becoming grown-ups, but for us it's amazing and upsetting. . . . We were not supposed to grow old: that's how we defined ourselves."

177

# notes

## i. reporting a generation

Page 15 **Marrying age:** U.S. Department of Census, 1992, 1993. Reported in "Grads Look for Stability," *The Boston Globe,* April 4, 1993; *The Washington Post,* April 18, 1993; *Newsweek,* April 5, 1993. David Aubrey explained to the *Minneapolis Star Tribune,* "Economically, it is not possible for a lot of young adults to get married and sustain themselves." "Tough Economic Times Produce a New Generation of Realists," *Minneapolis Star Tribune,* December 28, 1991.

Page 15 **Living at home:** U.S. Department of Census, 1993. Ages 22 to 24: 58 percent; ages 25 to 29: 30 percent; ages 30 to 34: 23 percent.

Page 15 **Unemployment:** "Twentysomething: What Happened to the American Dream?" ABC News, July 22, 1992; ABC put the number at 29.8 percent.

Page 15 **Income drop:** "Move Over, Boomers," *Business Week,* December 14, 1992: "According to the Center for Labor Market Studies at Northeastern University, the current median income for households headed by adults under 30 is $24,500. That's a 21% drop in constant dollars from 1973." "What Happened to the American Dream? The Under-30 Crowd May Be Losing the Race for Prosperity," *Business Week,* August 19, 1991: "On average, young men today earn 17% less, in inflation-adjusted terms, than they did in 1973." Neil Howe and William Strauss, *Generations* (New York: William Morrow, 1991), p. 327.

Page 16 **Housing costs:** Harvard University Joint Center For Housing Studies, 1990. Study also found that home ownership had fallen in same period, 20 percent for adults under 25 (from 23 percent in 1970 to 18 percent in 1990) and 20 percent for adults between 25 and 29 (44 percent to 35 percent).

Page 17 **Susan Faludi:** Susan Faludi, *Backlash* (New York: Crown, 1991). Faludi first made this point in the *Chicago Tribune.* Describing how a flawed Harvard-Yale study came to be perceived as the truth, Faludi wrote, "Like a national game of 'Telephone,' the story got increasingly muddled as it made the reportorial rounds. Speculation became fact. Predictions degenerated into foregone conclusions. And some information that was passed around was just plain wrong." "Single at 30," *Chicago Tribune,* December 21, 1986.

Page 18 **Subaru commercial:** "For Generation-X, the Angst Is On Line,"

*Los Angeles Times,* April 28, 1993. A year later, this spot was still the standard for poor niche marketing: "Subaru tried to stress the coolness of its Impreza model last year by featuring a sloppily dressed young actor who testified that the car was 'like punk rock,' while other brands were 'boring and corporate.' Perhaps this was designed to show how alienated young shoppers feel in the modern car culture. . . . The ad became a running joke among some members of the target audience and eventually Subaru switched agencies." Said one twenty-two-year-old marketing researcher, "[The] ad misses the mark because it portrays us as an idle generation, and we certainly do not perceive ourselves that way. Those of us who are struggling to make it are really struggling and working hard." "How Do You Turn On the Twentysomething Market?" *The New York Times,* April 17, 1994.

Page 18   **"The image"**: This image became so well established that *Esquire* could sum it up in a paragraph: "The Generation-X Guy: Do you loudly reject the false values of consumer society? Is this just a cheap excuse to laze around your parents' split-level, watching *House of Style?* Are marketers poring over Richard Linklater films desperate to divine your hopes, your dreams, and your preferences in a clear, fruit-based upmarket beverage? . . . Are you now or have you ever been a bike messenger?" "New American Stereotypes—1993," *Esquire,* January 1994.

Page 19   **" 'As they shield their eyes' "**: Neil Howe and William Strauss, "The New Generation Gap," *The Atlantic,* December 1992.

Page 19   **" 'Baby boomers see twentysomethings' "**: "Say Hello to America's Newest Lost Generation," *The Houston Chronicle,* April 4, 1993.

Page 20   **" 'job attitudes are veering from the old work ethic' "**: "The Squeeze on the Middle Class," *Business Week,* March 10, 1975.

Page 21   **" 'The activities of the generation as a whole remain considerably different' "**: "Why It's Called the 'Me' Generation," *U.S. News & World Report,* March 27, 1978.

Page 22   **_Time_ magazine**: "Proceeding with Caution," *Time,* July 16, 1990.

Page 24   **" 'what the middle class fears' "**: "But in the middle class there is another anxiety: a fear of inner weakness, of growing soft, of losing discipline and will." Barbara Ehrenreich, *Fear of Falling: The Inner Life of the Middle Class* (New York: Pantheon, 1989). p. 15.

Page 25   **"There had been any number"**: According to *The Economist, Time,* in the July 16, 1990 article "Proceeding with Caution," had "discovered" the baby bust. "Oh, Grow Up," *The Economist* (London), December 26, 1992.

Page 25   **Faludi:** Susan Faludi, *Backlash,* pp. 79, 81.

Page 26   **"the nation's fixation on money"**: "Getting By on $1 Million a Year," *Forbes,* October 27, 1986. ("If Dan had more money he would like a boat, or possibly a home in the islands. Vacations cost him $200,000 a year. Dan's wife is the force of moderation in the family.") Other articles on money: *New Republic* added the column "The Money Culture" in 1985; according to *The New York Times Magazine,* August 8, 1986, what we were seeing could be explained very simply: "Society's increasing preoccupation with wealth as a measure of achievement [is leading to] a fundamental shift in attitudes among the nation's brightest young people." "The Faster Track," *The New York Times Magazine,* August 8, 1986. From the heartland: "There's no shame in being social again, or rich, or fun-loving, or well-dressed." "The Good Life," the *Chicago Tribune,* December 17, 1986.

Page 27   **" 'the harsh, dry, materialistic wind' "**: Paul Johnson, "The Lost Ideals of Youth," *The New York Times,* March 25, 1984. Johnson, former editor of *The New Statesman,* explained, "Men and women maturing in the late 70's and early 80's are haunted by inflation. They have needed to earn money quickly just to survive."

Page 27   **Leavitt, 1985:** David Leavitt, "The New Lost Generation," *Esquire,* May 1985. "What is behind this skepticism? A need, I think, for settledness, for security. Our parents imagined they could satisfy this urge by marrying and raising children; our older brothers and sisters through community and revolution. We have seen how far those alternatives go."

Page 28   **"The reporters were astounded"**: William Rukeyser, "The Editor's Desk," *Fortune,* May 27, 1985.

Page 28   **"nail-biters and champion worrywarts"**: "The Baby Bust Hits the Job Market," *Fortune,* May 27, 1985. "Anyone who recalls college as a time of goofing off and enjoying youth would be astonished at the level of anxiety on campuses today. Most members of the class of '85 seem to have dedicated the past four years to assembling a list of credentials that would knock the socks off any recruiter they could get near." One student explained the high anxiety: "We all saw a time when money was tight."

Page 29  **Ellis at Bennington:** Bret Easton Ellis, "Down and Out at Bennington College: The Author of 'Less Than Zero' Ponders the New Stress on Success, the Slow Death of the Dreamer and the Lost Generation," *Rolling Stone,* October 1986.

Page 29  **"throughout the decade":** There was wide and anxious agreement about the new values of young people. "Kids are only interested in making money. . . . A high school junior pointed out his friends see success in terms of earning lots of money and owning lots of things. . . . Young people are being assaulted by the need to make it big, fast. They first want to be rich; then they decide what to do to get there." "Looking At a Limited Trust with a Child of a Child of the 60s," *Washington Post,* June 6, 1990. Also: "Money, money, money is the watchword of today. [Students] want to get out and make as much money as they can, to insure a cushion for the hard times they see as inevitable." "The Money Society," *Fortune,* July 6, 1987. See also: "Students Are All Business These Days," *Los Angeles Times,* November 14, 1988; "A Rising Tide of Materialism," *Washington Post,* February 1, 1986; "Why Feminism Failed," *The New York Times,* June 26, 1988 ("Studies show young people are turning to materialism like flies to butter"). Finally, Ellen Goodman: "Youth are on a fast track to materialism. . . . It's not that some spiritual flaw, some warped sense of values have infected this generation. If the young are preoccupied with money, power, status, it may be because they haven't been offered any better set of goals. By us." "Passing His Vision to a New Generation," *The Boston Globe,* November 22, 1988. For the shift in public perception, take Goodman's cartoon from graduation season 1988. "A cartoon from the last commencement season showed two college students crossing a campus. One is saying to the other, 'This is incredible. . . . Do you know that I, too, want as much as I can get as fast as I can get it?' " Compare with a version from 1994. A college president addresses the seniors. "Your alma mater wishes you much success as you take your next step into the future, whether that be grad school, social service, or your employer of choice." The students name that employer: "Gap!" "Gap!" "Gap!" "Kurt Cobain wore khakis!" "Doonesbury," Garry Trudeau, May 16, 1994.

Page 30  **"In *The Washington Post*":** Robert Samuelson, "The Media's

Fixation with Money," *The Washington Post,* October 15, 1986. "People who lived through the Depression or even today's young, who came of age in the shaky 1970s and 1980s, rarely had the innocent notions about money once nourished by older 'baby boomers.'" Samuelson also cleverly points out that Lee Iacocca—whose autobiography sold 2 million copies—"could not have become a folk hero a decade ago."

Page 30 "'ambitious overachievers'": "I Want to Do What Carl Ichan Does," *Forbes,* April 21, 1986.

Page 30 *The New York Times Magazine:* Bruce Weber, "The Unromantic Generation," *The New York Times Magazine,* April 5, 1987. Weber sounds like Leavitt: "I've come to think it ironic that in a youth-minded culture such as ours . . . those I spoke with seem largely restrained. Concerned with, if not consumed by, narrowing the options down, getting on track, they are aiming already at a distant comfort and security."

Page 31 *"Fortune* reiterated": "The Uncommitted Class of 1989," *Fortune,* June 5, 1989.

Page 32 **Enrollment:** "From Ban the Bomb to Benetton," *American Demographics,* September 1987. "Much of this change is understandable [in] an era of soaring college tuitions and shrinking student aid."

Page 32 "'**Meaningful philosophy**'": A. W. Astin et al., *The American Freshman: National Norms for Fall 1992* (Los Angeles: Higher Education Research Institute, UCLA), chart, p. 3.

Page 32 "**According to Roper CollegeTrack**": Himmelfarb, Roper CollegeTrack, as quoted in "The Uncommitted Class of 1989," *Fortune,* June 5, 1989.

Page 32 **sea change in the attitudes:** In fact, C. Evert Ladd, a demographic researcher, compared the baby bust with the baby boom and found there were few attitudinal changes even by the *decade.* "Serious magazines unapologetically publish drivel in what purports to be the latest entry in the American generational parade. . . . These silly assertions are, of course, left entirely unsubstantiated. . . . We reviewed recent data and reached the same conclusion. Neither the boomers nor the baby bust are 'profoundly different' generations [from earlier American generations]. Claims of sharp generational differences and conflict may make good copy, but they are rarely justified." "Twentysomething-Generation Myths Revisited," *The Public Perspective,* The Roper Center for Public Opinion, January 1994. Ladd directly addresses the vexing "work ethic" question: "Is the work ethic eroding as new generations appear on the scene? If it is, you can't tell it from surveys. The data don't show the work ethic stronger among older groups than among the young. The reasons people give for working—the cultural and social factors as well as the monetary ones—don't differ much from one group to another."

Page 34   **Job losses:** "Young Workers Are Bearing the Brunt of Layoffs," *Business Week,* December 10, 1990. Also, "What Happened to the American Dream?" *Business Week,* August 19, 1991.

Page 34   **Children's Defense Fund study:** "Closed-Door Generation," *Seattle Times,* January 10, 1992. "During the 1990–91 recession, workers younger than 25 absorbed nearly all of the job losses, according to a recent study by the Children's Defense Fund. . . . The study found that there were about a million fewer workers with jobs between January and May of 1991 as in the same period a year earlier. For those over 25, there was a net loss of only 164,000 jobs."

Page 34   **"According to the political writer":** William Greider, *Who Will Tell the People?* (New York: Simon and Schuster, 1991) pp. 81–82. "During the 1988 presidential campaign, George Bush comforted voters with a manly promise to enact 'no new taxes,' and his pledge resonated profitably with popular opinion. If voters had wished to know what George Bush would actually do as president, they should have been listening to other voices. An elite consensus of opinion leaders from both political parties . . . had already developed an agenda for what the next president should do to correct the economic imbalances created by the Reagan era."

Page 35   **"the spiritual life of Americans":** Ehrenreich, *Fear of Falling.* David Reisman made a similar point in *The Lonely Crowd* (New Haven: Yale University Press, 1950), p. 149, as early as 1950: "This attack against others as apathetic—as today, for instance, in the constant complaints over political and civic apathy—sometimes serves as a way of fighting against apathy in oneself." The anthropologist Karen Newman, reviewing Ehrenreich's book in *Psychology Today,* summarized, "Ehrenreich portrays the middle class as self-absorbed, unable to look beyond its own neuroses." "The Middle Class Neurosis," *Psychology Today,* October 1989.

Page 35   **" 'The baby busters are activists' ":** Editor's Note, "Meet the

Next Generation," *American Demographics,* April 1990. As Cheryl Russell, the magazine's editor, explained, "Once again, young adults believe they can control the course of their lives and the fate of their country."

Page 37 **Polling data:** Roper Poll, in "The Next Boom in Real Estate," *American Demographics,* May 1991; "Trading Power, Status, for the Simple Life," *Gannett News Service* August 30, 1991.

Page 37 **Careers; "two thirds of all employed Americans":** Brad Edmundson, "Remaking a Living," *Utne Reader,* July 1991. As Edmundson put it, "Americans hope to cut back on their work. It won't be easy, but it could be wonderful." Also "Time Out!" *Newsday,* July 11, 1993. *Fortune* discussed the shift away from the workplace in a cover story, "Pioneers of the New Balance," *Fortune,* May 20, 1991; also in "Burned-Out Boomers Flee to Families," *American Demographics,* December 1991 ("The signs are clear: In the 1990s, America's largest consumer group will place less emphasis on money and more on meaning.") Most completely articulated in *Time* cover story, "The Simple Life: Goodbye to Having It All," *Time,* April 8, 1991. A *Time*/CNN study found 69 percent of the people surveyed said they would like to "slow down and live a more relaxed life." In 1990, *Time* had differentiated "twentysomethings" by describing them as "a back-to-basics bunch that wishes life could be simpler." By 1991's "Simple Life," this was no longer a generation-specific attitude but the *nation's* attitude. "In place of materialism, many Americans are embracing simpler pleasures and homier values. They've been thinking hard about what really matters in their lives, and they've decided to make some changes. What matters is having time for family and friends, rest and recreation, good deeds and spirituality. . . . The pursuit of a simpler life with deeper meaning is a major shift in America's private agenda."

Page 38 **"the few groups who did *not* feel this way":** "What Young Americans Want," *American Demographics,* July 1991. "Young adults pursue a more materialistic version of the American Dream. Marriage and family remain important to the high school graduating class of 1986, but they are more likely than baby boomers to see money as the most important reason to work."

Page 38 **" 'less work' ethic":** "The Terrible Twenties," *Chicago Tribune,* February 13, 1992.

# notes

Page 38    " 'Grow Up, Crybabies' ": "Grow Up, Crybabies: You're America's Luckiest Generation," *The Washington Post,* September 12, 1993.

Page 38    **"A 'My Turn' "**: "The Whiny Generation," *Newsweek,* November 1, 1993.

Page 38    **"What has gotten into the brains of these kids?"**: "What 25-Year-Olds Want," *Fortune,* August 27, 1990. *Fortune* was so taken by *Time's* new tack that they repeated the new observations a year later, in "The Upbeat Generation," July 13, 1992: "They herald a back-to-basics movement"; *Time:* "While the recruiters are trying to woo young workers, a generation is out planning its escape from the 9-to-5 routine"; *Fortune,* 1992: "Rather than succumbing to societal pressure to find a job, stick with it, and build a career, legions of these young adults guiltlessly view their jobs as interludes between far-off adventures."

Page 39    **"statement was echoed"**: "Busters Have Work Ethic All Their Own," *USA Today,* July 20, 1993. Again, as *Time* had it, "They would rather hike in the Himalayas than climb the corporate ladder"; as *USA Today* had it, "As a group, the busters are clearly not interested in climbing the corporate ladder." Other *Time* sentences enjoyed similarly long half-lives: "AIDS casts a pall over a generation that fully expected to reap the benefits of the sexual revolution. Responsibility is the watchword." *The Boston Globe:* "Similarly, AIDS casts a pall over their sexual initiations." "Complaints of a New Generation; 'Baby Busters' Resent life in Boomers' Debris," November 10, 1991.

Page 39    " **'The twentysomethings are plentysomething' "**: "A Generation of Gripers . . . and How They Grew," *Psychology Today,* May 1992. The *New Work Force* book also suggested that under-thirty employees were "not as loyal to companies and employees as are older generations," though as early as 1989, in *Newsday,* the business writer Robert Kuttner had declared corporate loyalty among all groups to be a somewhat dicier issue: "The common theme of dozens of recent reports on American competitiveness is that the U.S. economy needs skilled, committed workers. Yet competitive pressures are driving industry to reduce costs by turning more and more employees into part-timers, or 'temps,' with little training, high turnover and scant reason to be loyal to their jobs." "The Hidden Costs of Hiring Those Cheap 'Temps,' " *Newsday,* May 25, 1989. So had *Fortune,* in 1988: "The old career-long marriage between employer and employee is giving way to a series of one-night stands." "Tomorrow's Jobs: Plentiful, But . . . ," *Fortune,* April 11, 1988.

Page 39 **1992 book:** Lawrence J. Bradford and Claire Raines, *Twentysomething: Managing and Motivating Today's New Work Force,* (MasterMedia Ltd., 1992).

Page 40 **The Conference Board's magazine:** "Here Come the Twentysomethings," *Across the Board,* May 1991. *Across the Board* also suggested adopting *Fortune's* 1990 name for the generation: "Yiffie," for young, individualistic, freedom-minded, and few, which sounds fun but is hard to say. The Human Resources publication *Personnel Journal* published its own hiring guide, in a cover story, "Managing the Baby Busters: Young Employees, Who Value Challenge and Growth More Than Money or Titles, Are Shaping a New Agenda for HR," *Personnel Journal,* March 1992. The subtitle takes one back to *Time* and to *Business Week* in 1975.

Page 40 " '**The negative labels'** ": Bob Guccione, Jr., "Unfair Play in the Generation Wars," *Los Angeles Times,* February 21, 1993. "Apathetic? More young people turned out to vote in November 1992 than ever before in this democracy. As for the alleged lack of ideals, the '60s people should take a look at their own . . . Young people are essentially no different than they have ever been. Only the conditions are different, as they always were. Young people are simply young and must go through what we people who are a little older had to go through: the process of learning about life."

Page 40 **"Fifty-five percent of all new job openings":** 1992 Northwestern University Lindquist-Endicott Survey, quoted in "Graduating to a Job Search: Grads Face Worst Market in 30 Years," *USA Today,* December 11, 1992.

Page 41 **"One young writer":** Richard Blow, "Twentynothing," *The Washington Post,* December 13, 1992. "Twentysomethings do have one constructive option: to reject the media hype and disband altogether."

Page 41 **Barbara Walters:** "Twentysomething: What Happened to the American Dream?" ABC News special, July 22, 1992.

Page 42 **"in need of basic repairs":** "The Repair Generation," *U.S. News & World Report,* February 2, 1993 (cover story); also "Post-Boomers: America's Clean-Up Brigade?" *USA Today,* May 6, 1993; "Good Examples In Capital," *Dallas Morning News,* April 26, 1993; Mary McGory in "Perchance, the 'Us' Decade?", *The Washington Post,* May 11, 1993: "In general, [this] acknowledges that we are all in this together." On the other hand, as William Greider demurred in "Smells Like Team Spirit," *Rolling Stone,* June 24, 1993, "National service points the finger in the wrong direction. The idea of responsibility does need to be addressed, but a better starting point is the failure of large institutions, both business and government, to confront their own behavior. . . . But it's a little unfair to expect the young to make good on the civic failure of their elders."

Page 44    **"In the fifties":** David Reisman, *The Lonely Crowd* (New Haven: Yale University Press, 1950), p. 164: "The uncertainty of life in our day is certainly a factor in the refusal of young people to commit themselves to long-term goals."

Page 44    **" 'become established' ":** Gustave Flaubert, *The Letters of Gustave Flaubert, Volume One.* (Cambridge, MA: Harvard University Press, 1980–1982), Francis Steegmuller, translator/editor, p. 130. Letter to Louis Bouilhet, November 14, 1950. "I am experiencing a need which everyone of our age feels to some extent with relation to society. I feel the need of 'becoming established.' "

Page 45    **"a *Newsweek* cover story":** John Leland, "The Billion Dollar Battle for Your Brain," *Newsweek,* October 11, 1993. Leland also made an extremely cogent remark about the baby bust in "Do You Hear What I Hear?" *Newsweek,* January 27, 1992: "This is the dilemma of the post-baby-boom generation. They've inherited truisms they know aren't true."

Page 47    **"The notion of 'selling out' ":** Ehrenreich addresses this, too. "I attended a meeting of a group dedicated to encouraging young people in the arts. When the question arose of whether to accept corporate sponsorship for a certain undertaking, there were many worried statements about "compromise". . . . Finally, someone rose to clarify the issue: The question is not whether we sell ourselves, he said, but whether we sell ourselves for a high enough price. Titters arose, in honor not only of the sexual innuendo, but of the larger resonance of his question." Ehrenreich, *Fear of Falling,* p. 247.

Page 48    **"Teenagers hoped":** "What Young Adults Want," *American Demographics,* July 1991. In fact, the proportions of teenage men and women who said it "was likely" they would marry and have children showed an increase for the baby bust class of 1986 over the baby boom class of 1976. "Both parenthood and marriage are more popular with the class of 1986 than they were in 1976." The source was the University of Michigan "Monitoring the Future" survey, which polls a "nationally representative" sample of high school seniors every year.

Page 48   " 'Developing a Meaningful Philosophy' ": A. W. Astin et al., *The American Freshman: National Norms for Fall 1993* (Los Angeles: Higher Education Research Institute, UCLA), p. 24. "Be Very Well Off Financially" had increased to 74.5 percent, nearly matching its 1987 high of 75.6 percent. "Develop Meaningful Philosophy of Life" had dropped to 44.6 percent, from 45.6 in 1992. All-time highs in the 1993 survey were recorded in "making money" as "very important" reason for attending college (75.1 percent, compared with 73.3 percent in 1992 and 49.9 percent in 1971), "to get a better job" (82.1 percent, 78.5 percent in 1992 and 71 percent in 1970). Say Astin et al., "The results of the survey also reveal that students are more concerned than ever about financial issues."

## ii. the bottom of all that americans do

Page 53   " 'Golden Opportunities' ": "The Baby Bust Hits the Job Market," *Fortune,* May 27, 1985. "By the time the class of 1989 comes along . . . graduates will face less competition for jobs and, later, for promotions. Demographers and economists forecast golden opportunities for the class of 1989 and for those that follow until the mid-90s. . . . After 15 years of glut, college graduates will be back in the catbird seat, able [to] watch the butterflies. Soon it will be employers' turn to worry."

Page 56   **"quotations"**: Such stories were often given a sweetly comic ring. "After four long years of grueling coursework in physics at a competitive engineering college, Dean O'Donnell landed a job as a singing banana. The closest O'Donnell comes to putting his degree from Worcester Polytechnic Institute to use is pumping helium into a dozen, 16-inch, jumbo helium balloons in less than four minutes as part of his job delivering those balloons. "I am the most highly educated singing gorilla in Boston," laughed O'Donnell. . . . The pressure from parents and friends barely affects O'Donnell, according to him, but many graduates say the jokes about their lack of jobs soon become tiresome, and the family pressures mount with each rejected resume." "The Year After," *The Boston Globe,* May 24, 1990.

Page 56   " **'We were told' "**: "Move Over, Boomers," *Business Week,* December 14, 1992.

Page 58   **Easterlin:** Richard Easterlin, *Birth and Fortune* (New York: Basic Books, 1979).

Page 58   " **'As for the baby bust generation,' "**: "Population Changes that Help for a While," *Business Week,* September 9, 1979. Professor Robert Wachter, a colleague of Easterlin's: "From the standpoint of demographic trends, the next two decades will provide a golden opportunity for economic progress."

Page 58   **"In the mid-eighties, magazines"**: "The Generation That Is Getting Less of the Pie," *Business Week,* September 15, 1980; *Fortune,* "Baby Bust Hits Job Market"; "In Praise of Children," *Newsweek,* January 13, 1986; " 'Baby Bust' Expected to Have a Profound Impact on U.S. Economy," *The Washington Post,* January 18, 1988 ("Their smaller number should bid up wage levels and raise disposable incomes"); "The Baby Bust; Coming of Age," *The National Journal,* March 8, 1986 ("Many economists predict bidding wars for baby bust workers, who could end up with substantial pay increases"); "The Prime of Our Lives," *Psychology Today,* May 1987 ("Compared with the baby boomers, the smaller cohort just approaching adulthood 'will have much more favorable experiences as they grow up—in their families, in school and finally in the labor market,' he [Easterlin] says. As a result, they will 'develop a more positive psychological outlook.' "); "The Lost-Out Generation," *Los Angeles Times,* October 18, 1988 ("Ironically, the same phenomenon that has held back baby boomers is going to help the next demographic group made up of baby busters. One economist says, 'These are the kids who probably all their lives are going to walk down the street and see half a dozen help-wanted signs.' ") Even as late as 1994, a magazine reader could still encounter this prediction, as with Jane Bryant Quinn, writing in "The Myth of Generation X," *Newsweek,* June 6, 1994.

Page 58   " **'The skimpier the generation' "**: "Snapshot of a Changing America," *Time,* September 2, 1985.

Page 58   " **'higher salaries and more responsibility' "**: "Welcome, America, to the Baby Bust," *Time,* February 23, 1987. Also, "When the baby-bust generation enters adulthood, it may discover the benefits of doing without: without as much unemployment, without as much demand for housing or cutthroat competition for good jobs, possibly even without as much crime."

Page 59  **Age for first marriages:** U.S. Census, 1993. 24.4 for women, 26.5 for men.

Page 59  **Size of families:** "Census Bureau Reports Dramatic Changes in Families," *San Francisco Chronicle,* December 7, 1989: The average family was 3.7 people in 1960; it was 3.16 in 1989. "The size of the average American family this year reached an all-time low for the post-war era, the federal government will report today. . . . The study also revealed that people in the so-called Baby Bust generation born after 1965 are waiting longer to set up their own households. . . . U.S. families in 1989 averaged only 3.16 people, the smallest size since 1940 when such statistics began to be collected, according to the Census Bureau study, which was based on a national survey. . . . People in the baby bust generation are also taking longer to strike out on their own. 'Today's young adults are not forming their own households at as high a rate as in earlier years. This may either be a matter of personal preference or economic necessity,' the report noted." Also from "U.S. Households Shrinking: 1 in 4 Americans Now Lives Alone, 1990 Census Finds," *Atlanta Journal-Constitution,* May 1, 1991: " 'I think the overriding story average household size tells us is delayed marriage, delayed family formation,' said Carl Haub, a demographer with the Population Reference Bureau in Washington. . . . These changes [have] changed some basic assumptions about American families. The proportion of households composed of married couples with at least one child fell from 40% in 1970 to 26% in 1990, according to an annual Census Bureau survey."

Page 59  **Lower incomes:** "Move Over Boomers," *Business Week,* December 14, 1992. In "What Happened to the American Dream," *Business Week,* August 19, 1991, the Center for Labor Market Studies had put the figure at 17 percent. In the same period, for parents under 25, incomes fell by nearly one half. See also *Money,* "The American Dream and Today's Reality," October 1992. In *Boiling Point* (New York: Random House, 1993), p. 191, Kevin Phillips draws on the work of Professor Frank Levy of MIT and Robert C. Michel of the Urban Institute. "Some of the statistics are extraordinary. Back in 1950 the average thirty-year-old man would have added 58 percent more pay by the time he reached forty, and in 1960 his successor would have added 44 percent. By contrast, the thirty-year-old of 1977 had gained only 21 percent more by 1987." The *Atlanta Journal-Constitution,* July 3, 1992: "As evidence of how tough it's been so far for the younger generation, [the] number of full-time employees 16 or older who earned less than $12,-195 almost doubled, from 7.8 million in 1979 to more than 14 million in 1990." In a recent article, *The Atlantic* gave further numbers about income drops for the generation: "Among young males aged 18-to-24 who worked full time, the percentage earning less than $12,195 (in 1990 dollars) a year more than doubled during the 1980s, from 18 to 40. Among young women, the percentage earning less than $12,195 a year increased from 29 to 48." "Who Speaks for the Middle Class?" *The Atlantic,* May 1994. The numbers on health insurance are similar: "Young people make up the largest group of uninsured in the nation, according to a recent study by Families USA, a Washington-based health consumer group. About 38 percent of all Americans between the ages of 18 and 30—more than 16 million individuals—have no insurance." "For Many, Health Insurance Goes When Graduation Day Arrives," *The Boston Globe,* March 3, 1993.

Page 59   **Jobs in sixties and seventies:** "1980's Grads: Baby Boom to Job Bust," *The New York Times,* October 16, 1983. "In the eighties, only 28% of the new jobs will be in these high-level occupations. There will be 13 times as many jobs for waiters and waitresses as jobs for aeronautical engineers and three times as many jobs for janitors as for computer-systems analysts."

Page 59   **Leaders in job creation:** Wal-Mart created 325,000 jobs in the eighties, UPS 138,000 jobs. "Job Picture," *Money,* April 1993. "The greatest job opportunities during the 1980s were at much less glitzy companies."

Page 59   **Underemployment in eighties:** *Monthly Labor Review* (Bureau of Labor Statistics), July 1992, "Reconciling Data on Jobs for College Graduates" and "The Future of Jobs for College Graduates." "Data sources also suggest that there were more college graduates than there were openings in college-level jobs during the 1980s. . . . BLS projects this divergence will continue through 2005." "Interpreting Conditions in the Job Market for College Graduates," *Monthly Labor Review,* June,

1993, repeats these findings and concludes, "These projections should be of great concern to policy makers. . . . In this economic environment, what are the implications that the poor labor market for college graduates is likely to get worse?" According to "A Degree of Reality," *USA Today,* June 2, 1993, "That prediction may already be coming true: One-third of 9,000 '91 and '92 graduates surveyed by MSU's Collegiate Employment Research Institute held jobs that didn't require degrees, up from 15% five years ago."

Page 61    **"870,000 new American payroll jobs"**: "Jobs Go to the Lucky Few: College Seniors Face Daunting Road to Employment," *The Boston Globe,* May 2, 1993. Graduating classes from 1991 to 1993 were in excess of one million students per year.

Page 61    **"Britainization of America"**: "The Morning After," Pete Peterson, *The Atlantic,* October, 1987; Kevin Phillips, *The Politics of Rich and Poor* (New York: Random House, 1990); Phillips, *Boiling Point* (New York: Random House, 1993).

Page 62    **"According to *Success*"**: Martin Amis, *Success,* pp. 34, 181, 183.

Page 63    **" 'depression levels' "**: "1980's Grads: Baby Boom to Job Bust," *The New York Times,* October 16, 1983. " 'It was a year of "depression levels" of unemployment in their peer group,' wrote Victor R. Lindquist."

Page 63    **" 'Job openings at individual firms will be down' "**: "Turn for Better in Job Prospects for '84 Grads," *U.S. News & World Report,* December 12, 1983.

Page 63    **" 'The class of '88 is in luck' "**: "First Job: Moving out of the Classroom," *U.S. News & World Report,* April 25, 1988; also, "In Demand: the Class of '88," *Time,* May 23, 1988: "The nearly 1 million U.S. college seniors who will don cap and gown in the next few weeks could not have picked a more propitious time to be venturing out of ivy-covered campuses and into the workaday world. Says one head of career counseling, 'I've never seen students more job conscious than they are today.' "

Page 63    **" 'It's going to be quite competitive' "**: "Tough Times for Most College Grads," *Fortune,* August 13, 1990. "Several major players have taken themselves out of the job market."

Page 63    **" 'worst year since 1945' "**: "Graduating College Seniors Face

## notes

School of Hard Knocks," *The Washington Post,* May 5, 1991. Counselor is Patricia Carretta, director of George Mason's Career Development Center.

Page 64  **"into year 2005":** Kristina J. Shelley, "The Future of Jobs for College Graduates," *Monthly Labor Review,* July 1992, pp. 15, 17, 19; Lindquist tells the *Los Angeles Times:* "It's probably the worst I've seen in the 30 years that I've been in the business," "The Job Scramble: Employment Prospects For Class of '92 May Be Worst In A Generation," *Los Angeles Times,* October 12, 1992; "Graduating to a Job Search: Grads Face Worst Market in 30 Years," *USA Today,* December 11, 1992: "According to a new [Lindquist] report by Northwestern University, companies hired 56% more college grads in 1988 than they did this year."

Page 64  **College Placement Council:** "Job-Hunt Strategy for New Grads," Cleveland *Plain Dealer,* June 10, 1993. "This is not something temporary. This is the wave of the future. . . . Companies are hiring experienced workers to meet their entry-level needs because it is cost-effective."

Page 64  **Karen Newman:** "Busting the American Dream," *The New York Times,* May 16, 1993.

Page 64  **"classes were now one third larger":** 965,000 in 1983, 1.3 million in 1993. "Have Degree, Will Travel; the Class of '83 Faces the Worst Job Prospects Since World War II," *Time,* June 6, 1983; "Current Crop of College Graduates Finds Job Market Painfully Tight," *The New York Times,* June 6, 1993. "Graduates Facing Worst Prospects in Last 2 Decades," *The New York Times,* May 12, 1992. Combining the first and last suggests that these are the worst job prospects since before World War II.

Page 65  **Bad choices:** American Demographics wrote on this in "Why the Baby Bust Won't Spend," December 1992: "College students are supposed to have the brightest prospects, but even they 'are in a panic,' says Pamela Gardiner, interim director of career development at the University of Vermont. 'They also feel tremendous guilt because they are supposed to be able to get jobs.' "

Page 65  **"Was it easier to get a job":** Lindquist, in the *Houston Chronicle,* April 4, 1993: "It's probably the worst—the last two years were the worst—in the last 30 years." Similarly, from *Monthly Labor Review,* July 1992: "During the 1960s, employers heavily recruited college graduates. Few graduates, regardless of their field of study, had difficulty finding college-level jobs. Jobs sought graduates."

Page 66  " '**They simply don't know how to get hired**' ": "It Takes More Than a Degree," *Forbes,* December 3, 1984; Steve Finnegan in "I Want to Do What Carl Ichan Does," *Forbes* April 21, 1986.

Page 68  **Weidenbaum:** Quoted in Sidney Blumenthal, "The Sorcerer's Apprentices," *The New Yorker,* July 19, 1993.

Page 69  **Carter:** "The U.S. Bias Against Savings," *Business Week,* December 11, 1978. "This means that if the Administration bends its goal of a balanced budget and opts for the old Keynesian quick fix [of deficit spending] in the pursuit of a short-term burst of economic activity, it could cost the nation years of slower long-run growth, slumping productivity, and further loss of international competitiveness." Fears were then expressed about $50 billion deficits. See also "A One-Martini Toast to the Carter Program," *Fortune,* February 27, 1978. Carter's $61 billion is called "a huge deficit." There is also "hope that the new congressional budget procedure will help keep the deficit from spinning out of control."

Page 69  **James Coleman:** "Role of Young Adults in the Years Ahead," *U.S. News & World Report,* March 27, 1978.

Page 69  **Lasch on future:** Christopher Lasch, *The Culture of Narcissism: American Life in an Age of Diminishing Expectations* (New York: Norton, 1979), pp. 23, 26, 30; "The society has lost interest in the young and in posterity" (p. 365).

Page 70  " ' **"Earn the maximum for the minimum"** ' ": "The Terrible Twenties," *Chicago Tribune,* February 13, 1992.

Page 70  **Stockman:** Sidney Blumenthal, "The Sorcerer's Apprentices," *The New Yorker,* July 19, 1993.

Page 71  **"Stockman told *The Atlantic*":** "Education of David Stockman," *The Atlantic,* December 1981, an interview with William Greider. Greider carefully details the 1981 tax legislation in Chapter 3 of *Who Will Tell The People* (and comes out sounding much like Stockman): "The orgy of 1981 defined everything that has followed since. The perennial tax debate is still preoccupied with finding ways to correct the embarrassing excesses of Reagan's tax legislation and reduce the huge deficits that 'supply-side' economics created" (p. 92).

Page 72  **"Reading the debate of that time":** For example, this from the

"Week In Review" section of *The New York Times:* "Q. What is a budget deficit? A. An excess of spending over tax receipts. Q. How does the Treasury get the money to cover that excess? A. It borrows, by selling Treasury securities to people and institutions with money to lend, investors . . . Q. What's bad about that? A. That depends on whom you ask. In the 1950s, President Dwight D. Eisenhower, a Republican, said the accumulated debt—known as the national debt—was a burden on future generations. . . . Mr. Reagan says deficits are preferable to tax increases. Q. What did General Eisenhower mean about deficits being a burden on the next generation? A. He meant that the debt would have to be paid off, and that the money would have to come from taxes. Q. Wasn't he right? A. It doesn't look that way." "Just How Serious Are Deficit Dangers?" *The New York Times,* October 23, 1983. For a revision, see "Reagan's Revenge," *The New York Times Magazine,* June 19, 1994

Page 72    **"The economics of joy"**: Herbert Stein, "A Dangerous Time for Economic Policy," *Fortune,* December 27, 1982.

Page 73    **Grace ads:** The two ads are described in "It's a Crying Shame," *Newsweek,* December 10, 1984; "Grace Advertises Gloomy Future," *Business Week,* February 12, 1986; "The Trials of 2017 A.D.," *Time,* February 10, 1986.

Page 73    **"prodigal parents"**: Governor Richard Lamm, "Borrowing from Our Children," *The Christian Science Monitor,* May 29, 1985.

Page 74    **Rauch:** *The Atlantic,* quoted in *Harvard Business Review,* "America's Debts and Deficits," July 1989.

Page 74    **Pete Peterson:** Pete Peterson, "The Morning After," *The Atlantic,* October 1987.

Page 75    **GDP, red ink:** These numbers come from "Budget For Fiscal Year 1994," the Congressional Budget Office, Historical Tables. Table 1.1—Summary of Receipts, Outlays, and Surpluses or Deficits: 1789–1998; Table 1.2—Summary of Receipts, Outlays, and Surpluses or Deficits as Percentages of GDP: 1934–1998, pp. 13–16.

Page 76    **William Branson:** Quoted in "The Burden of Debt: Why Economists Fear the Deficit," *The New York Times,* May 26, 1992. " 'We used to think the long-term growth rate was 3 percent. Now, an optimistic growth rate is 2 percent.' The difference, [Branson] said, is the drag from debt."

Page 76 **"They simply cannot find work"**: "Young People Could Rock the Vote," *Chicago Tribune,* October 19, 1992. "A college degree, which used to represent a one-way ticket to a better life, no longer even guarantees a job sufficient to pay back college loans. 'My friends who have graduated from school right now don't know what to do,' says Kate Frucher. 'They simply cannot find work.' "

Page 77 **" 'party' analogy"**: Most fully articulated in Michael Featherman, "The 80's Party Is Over . . . " *The New York Times,* September 24, 1990: "Odd, then, that now that the party's over, we should get stuck with the bill." Also in: "Till Death Do Us Part," *San Diego Union-Tribune,* August 8, 1992 ("Author Coupland: 'Some nights I lie awake in fear that my generation was handed a broom and told to sweep up after the baby boomer's party.' "); *American Demographics,* April 1993 ("In the eyes of young adults, boomers had a party and didn't clean up the mess."); *The Washington Post,* May 12, 1991; *Money,* August 1991. Most baroquely articulated by William Howe in "Generations: the Times of Our Lives," *Los Angeles Times,* April 4, 1991: "Howe adds that because 13ers are coming of age at a more sobering time than the boomers, they feel as if they've come upon a beach trashed from a summer of partying. And they get fined for littering."

Page 77 **" 'The most common opening' "**: "Is College Worth It?" *Forbes,* February 13, 1984.

Page 77 **" 'no golden ticket' "**: "Pros Join Entry-Level Chase," *Chicago Tribune,* July 4, 1993.

Page 77 **" 'Go ahead, take a short-term job' "**: "Job-Hunt Strategy for New Grads," Cleveland *Plain Dealer,* June 10, 1993. Also, "Graduates Forced To Change Course," *Houston Chronicle,* June 2, 1992: "If a student cannot find an opening somehow related to his or her field, Small [vice president of Student Services, University of Houston] advises accepting temporary work or a job at a fast food place."

Page 78 **" 'Volunteer at a nonprofit' "**: "Three Tips to Help New Grads Land a First Job," *Money,* March 1992.

### iii. the disappearance of childhood

Page 82 **" 'fragile hot-house egos' "**: "The Clinging Kid," *Money,* June 1988.

# notes

Page 83 **The American standard of living in 1973:** The most well-known proponents of this theory are MIT economists Frank S. Levy and Urban Institute member Robert Michel, coauthors of *The Economic Future of American Families: Income and Wealth Trends* (Washington, D.C.: Urban Institute Press, 1991). By their calculations, at the end of WWII, the average family income in the United States in today's dollars was $14,000. For the next thirty years, family incomes grew steadily, doubling by 1973. Then, after the first OPEC oil price hike, wages suddenly stopped growing and productivity faltered. Today's average family income is no higher than that of twenty years ago. Levy and Michel are discussed in Robert Kuttner, "The Patrimony Society," *New Republic,* May 11, 1987; Phillips, *Boiling Point;* Katherine Newman, *Withering Fortunes* (New York: Basic Books, 1993). The concept appears in Thomas Byrne Edsall, "The Return of Inequality," *The Atlantic,* June 1988; also, "Why We're So Gloomy," *Time,* January 13, 1992: "Says Allen Sinai, chief economist of the Boston Company: 'The 1973 period marked the beginning of the decline of the American standard of living. The Reagan years interrupted that trend by borrowing and spending, which lead to the retrenchment that has deepened the current slump.' "

Page 83 *"better,* **easier, more** *natural"*: Susan Littwin, *The Postponed Generation* (New York: William Morrow, 1986). Littwin repeatedly makes the point that talk shows and how-to articles made modern parents uneasy about their roles, in a way they had not been in the fifties: "What the child care experts did do, at least indirectly, was create the idea of the professional parent. With all of this advice available on television talk shows and in magazines and paperback books, raising children could no longer be something that you did by tradition or whim or common sense" (p.22).

Page 83 " **'One book complained'** ": "1970s-era children went from a family culture of *My Three Sons* to *My Two Dads*": Howe and Strauss, *Generations* (New York: William Morrow, 1991), p. 329.

Page 83 **"Go back to the fifties"**: Reisman, *The Lonely Crowd.* An interesting comparison with Littwin thirty years later: "The parents also have their sources of direction in the mass media. For in their uneasiness as to how to bring up children they turn increasingly to books, magazines, government pamphlets, and radio programs. . . . Moreover, the parents no longer feel themselves superior to the children. Within their own homes, [children] are the privileged guests in a rather second-rate hotel whose harassed but smiling managers they put under constant pressure for renovation" (pp. 70, 76).

Page 84   **Lasch:** Christopher Lasch, *The Culture of Narcissism,* pp. 267–317. Lasch includes this bit of 1931 anxiety about child rearing, again sounding very much like the 1980s: "The severe criticism of the average mother's way with her children coming from social workers, psychiatrists, and educators has helped to destroy a great complacency which was formerly the young mother's protection. The dictum that 'mother knows best' and the dogma of the natural instincts of motherhood have so fallen in disfavor as to be available refuges only for the ignorant or the stubborn." Nor was there "certainty" during WWI. He quotes *Good Housekeeping,* 1914: " 'Instinct tells a mother what to do.' Oh, it's an old chant, and it is as scientific as the classic statement that the moon is made of green cheese" (p. 279).

Page 84   **Letter from 1911:** Howe and Strauss, "The New Generation Gap," *The Atlantic,* December 1992. In *13th Gen* (New York: Vintage, 1993), they suggest their attitude toward their twentysomething audience: "You wouldn't be reading this if everything we said came with a long footnote" (p. 158).

Page 84   **"Working mothers probably rarer":** Barbara Dafoe Whitehead, "Dan Quayle Was Right," *The Atlantic,* April 1993. Victor Fuchs, in *How We Live* (Cambridge: Harvard University Press, 1983), puts the numbers higher. "In 1965 only 12% of married women with children under six years of age were wage-earners; by 1980 the proportion had soared to 45%." As Fuchs puts it, "The raw statistics of recent decades suggest that Americans have been caught up in a whirlpool of social change" (p. 1).

Page 85   **"destabilized to an enormous degree":** "Role of Young Adults in the Years Ahead," *U.S. News & World Report,* March 27, 1978.

Page 85   **"altering the nature of the family":** Fuchs, *How We Live:* "Dramatic changes in rates of marriage [and] divorce have led some observers to predict the end of the family as we know it" (p. 140).

Page 87   **Divorce rate:** "Dan Quayle Was Right," *The Atlantic,* 1993.

Page 87   **"In the full global competition":** "The American Dream and Today's Reality," *Money,* October 1992. Howe and Strauss put the rate higher. They cite a National Center for Health Statistics study showing a quadrupling in the divorce rate between 1970 and 1986.

Page 87    **"time when parents were disappearing"**: Parental time available to children "fell appreciably—10 hours less per week—between 1960 and 1986." Sylvia Ann Hewlett, *When the Bough Breaks: The Cost of Neglecting Our Children* (New York: Basic Books, 1991) quoted in Barbara Dafoe Whitehead, "The New Family Values," *Utne Reader,* May 1993.

Page 87    **Postman:** Neil Postman, *The Disappearance Of Childhood* (New York: Viking, 1981). As Postman puts it, "The charm, malleability, innocence and curiosity of children [is] degraded and then transmogrified into the lesser features of pseudo-adulthood."

Page 88    " **'certain facets'** ": "TV's 'Disastrous' Impact on Children," interview with Neil Postman, *U.S. News & World Report,* January 19, 1981. Postman continues, "Even more serious, in my view, is that television is opening up all of society's secrets and taboos, thus erasing the dividing line between childhood and adulthood and leaving a very homogenized culture in its wake."

Page 88    **TV hours:** Postman, in *The Disappearance of Childhood,* calculates the number of viewing hours as 15,000. By 1992, ABC News would calculate the number as 23,000.

Page 88    " **'Parents proudly urge children'** ": Elizabeth Crow, "Where Have All the Children Gone?" *The Washington Post,* August 15, 1982.

Page 90    " **'I think television has served a very useful function'** ": "Junior Knows Best: TV's View of Children Today," *The New York Times,* September 19, 1982. The article describes a scene from *Silver Spoons:* "When Ricky tries to engage his father in a serious discussion, Edward flops to his knees to demonstrate his favorite game, Swamp Wars. Asked by Ricky if the computer controlling their household gadgets has a 'random access memory,' Edward is the picture of slack-jawed bewilderment."

Page 91    **Sex, alcohol:** The figure on eleventh-grade sex comes from a University of Wisconsin study reported in "A Much Riskier Passage," *Newsweek* Special Issue, June 1990. The figures on alcohol and jobs appear in "Growing Up Too Fast; Experts Warn That Children Are Being Pushed to Act Like Adults Long Before They Are Ready," the *Los*

*Angeles Times,* August 9, 1988. As the paper continues: "In fact, the portrait of today's child—dressed from birth to look like a miniature adult, pressured to read before kindergarten and left unsupervised after school—is causing alarm among some psychologists who suggest the push to make children grow up quickly is symptomatic of an underlying societal disregard for their well-being. 'There are times in history when children fare better than others,' said David Elkind. 'But there's no question about it: children are not well cared for in our society.'"

Page 92   **Indiana study:** "Growing Up Too Fast," *Los Angeles Times.*

Page 94   **Hazel:** "The Kids Take Over: The Child of the 90s Cleans the House, Looks After Siblings, and Does the Grocery Shopping While Mom and Dad Are at Work," *Atlanta Journal-Constitution,* June 7, 1993. As the article explained, "Many Americans' children and teenagers have been transformed into caretakers by the rapid social changes of the past two decades, trends that have affected all races and classes." Nearly three quarters of all Southern children live in one-parent, one-worker homes or two-parents, two-worker homes.

Page 94   **The new childhood:** For another comparison of adolescence in the fifties and sixties versus adolescence today, see teen literature. "The crammed [bookstore] shelves are lined with florescent spines bearing titles like *Don't Look Behind You, Last Act, Bury Me Deep* [and] *The Slumber Party Massacre.* . . . I'd argue that the books are now cruder and ruder because the future prospects for today's teenagers aren't as merry as they were for all their Nancy-Drew-and-Hardy-Boys-reading baby boom parents. . . . Francessca Lia Block's weirdly sweet *Weetzie Bat* is about a cheeky L.A. teenage girl who creates her own family by having a child with her two gay male roommates (they had a ménage à trois, so that everyone would feel equally involved). This punk fairy tale makes the books that I took to the bathtub look like, well, kid stuff." "Are You There Freddy? It's Me, Heather: A Tour of the Sometimes Terrifying World of Teen Fiction," *Utne Reader,* July 1993. See also "Carnage: An Open Book," *Time,* August 2, 1993.

Page 95   **" 'After the split' ":** "The Price They Pay," *The New York Times Magazine,* February 18, 1990.

Page 96   **Tom Robinson:** Harper Lee, *To Kill a Mockingbird* (New York: Warner, 1982), p. 197. "The witness realized his mistake and shifted uncomfortably in the chair. But the damage was done."

## notes

Page 97 **Divorce statistics:** "Dan Quayle Was Right," *The Atlantic,* April 1993. "Only eleven percent of children born in the fifties would by the time they turned eighteen see their parents separate or divorce." By the 1990s, a reverse. "By the close of this decade, fewer than 3 of 10 kids will have lived in a continuously intact family until the age of 18." Katherine Boo, "Grow Up, Twenty-Somethings, You Can Go Home Again," *Washington Monthly,* April 1992.

Page 97 **"one in three marriages":** "Living Together," *Newsweek,* August 1, 1977.

Page 97 **"one million divorces a year":** "The Unromantic Generation," *The New York Times Magazine;* number was unchanged as of 1993, in "Dan Quayle." Suzanne M. Bianchi, of the Census Bureau, reports: "Since 1972, more than 1 million children each year have seen their parents divorce, a threefold increase since 1950. But the *percentage* of children whose parents divorce has risen even faster. In the 1950s, only 6 out of every 1,000 children experienced parental divorce in a given year, but in the 1980s, this rate varied between 17 and 19 per 1,000." *American's Children: Mixed Prospects* (Population Reference Bureau, 1990), reprinted in William Dunn's *The Baby Bust* (New York: American Demographics Books, 1993), p. 28.

Page 97 **"The number of 'latchkey kids' tripled":** "Through the 1970s, 12 percent of elementary school children and 30 percent of middle school kids were latchkey children, triple the rate of the previous decade." "Just Fix It!," *U.S. News & World Report,* February 22, 1993.

Page 97 **"guides":** *Your Child: The Latchkey Years* (Des Moines: Better Homes and Gardens Books, 1990), pp. 44–61. The introduction explains that the book will be full of "no-nonsense suggestions."

Page 98 **Parents, mid-eighties families:** By the mid-eighties, only 28.5 percent of all households consisted of husband, wife, and children, and "the stereotypical nuclear family of mom, dad and two kids now accounts for only 11% of all households." "Snapshot of a Changing America," *Time,* September 2, 1985. As the magazine explains, " 'Typical' is no longer an adjective that can describe the American household."

Page 98 **Single parents:** 10 percent in 1970 to 20 percent in 1982. "Baby Bust: Coming of Age," *National Journal,* March 8, 1986. As of 1992, 30 percent of children live with only one parent. "The American Dream and Today's Reality," Money, October 1992. Information about the drop in income appears in "Mothers and Divorce," *Psychology Today,* January 1987, and is updated in "Quayle," *The Atlantic,* April 1993. The NCHS study appears in the same magazine.

Page 98  **Ellen Goodman:** Ellen Goodman, "The Children in the Man-Woman Crisis," *The Boston Globe,* April 6, 1989.

Page 98  " **'a proxy situation'** ": "These young adults also assumed the role of proxies. . . . After their parents had parted, some of those surveyed recalled allowing themselves to return to a recently relinquished parent-child relationship. . . . Others described a quasi-symbiotic relationship with one or the other parent in which both parent and child were by turns both host and parasite. Though many felt compelled to rescue their parents, several baldly stated that they deeply resented the 'hysterical calls in the middle of the night,' the incessant ruminations about 'the same old stuff.' It is noteworthy, however, that those who were enraged by parental pleas and demands felt, nonetheless, obliged to leave school at times and comfort the beleaguered parent at home. As a young woman stated succinctly, 'If I stayed at school, I was worried about my Mom; if I went home I was worried about me.' " "The Price They Pay," *The New York Times Magazine,* February 18, 1990. Also, Lawrence Kutner, "Parent and Child," *The New York Times,* October 2, 1991. "They may alternate parental roles depending upon the situation. . . . In some families [there] is a mirror image of the old dependency, this time with the parent dependent upon the child." A therapist warned that difficulties might occur "when a parent is inappropriately using the adolescent as a main source of emotional support. When the child is young, it feels good. But when the child enters adolescence and would ordinarily start separating from the parents, this turns them into caricatures of adults. They have the responsibility without the independence." See also "Parent and Child," *The New York Times,* May 23, 1991.

Page 98  " **'At my father's wedding'** ": Patricia Thomas, letter to the editor, "The Price They Pay," *The New York Times Magazine,* March 11, 1990.

Page 104  **"One psychologist told":** "The Younger Generation That Never Grew Up," *Los Angeles Times,* April 17, 1986. Neil Postman had a wicked comment on this in "Has Road to Adulthood Suddenly Gotten Longer?" *The Christian Science Monitor,* March 13, 1986. "If one says things like marriage or so-called adult responsibilities are being postponed, the fact is that adults don't take those responsibilities seriously themselves anymore. Adults already dress like the young. They like the same music and movies as the young. They don't vote any more in any greater percentage than the young. So that while there is a sort of postponement of theoretical adult responsibilities, the point has to be raised as to whether or not these responsibilities that are being postponed mean anything to the adult world."

Page 104   **Susan Littwin book:** Littwin, *The Postponed Generation,* pp. 115, 141. Littwin continues: "As a group, [80s kids] had the most attentive parents in the world, and life's wrinkles were always smoothed away."

Page 105   " **'How is it that' ":** Reisman, *The Lonely Crowd,* p. 18.

## iv. indentured students

Page 109   **Student debt:** The College Board. The most recent year for which official numbers are available is 1989–90, when the average cumulative debt was $9,744. The study was conducted by the National Center for Education Statistics, at the U.S. Department of Education. In 1989–90, the debt ceiling (the maximum amount a student may borrow over a four-year period) was $12,000—it has increased rapidly since then, and in 1994 stood at $17,500. By 1993, newspapers were routinely speaking of $65,000 debts for law students ("Better by Degrees; College Grads Seeking Career Edge by Staying in School," *Newsday,* May 9, 1993) and medical students ("Future Doctors Unsettled by Health-Care Changes," *The New York Times,* April 9, 1993). As early as 1987 ("The Patrimony Society," *The New Republic,* May 11, 1987) Robert Kuttner could write, "in the case of postgraduate degree holders, the average debt is some $30,000."

Page 111   **College expansion, storm cloud:** "Colleges depend on an endless supply of 18-year-old recruits. . . . Baby boomers turned higher education into a multibillion-dollar business that employed more people than the automobile industry. Now universities will have to scale back." "Snapshot," *Time,* September 2, 1985. (See also note to page 121, "a good deal to fear.") There was some disagreement over the number. In "Denver University Reshapes Itself to Weather 'Baby Bust' '80s and '90s," *The Christian Science Monitor,* March 8, 1985: "There are not enough tuition-paying, 18–22 year-olds to go around. Demographics predict a 25% drop in this age group over the next decade, as the number of high school graduates skids from a 1977 high of 3.15 million to 2.3 million in 1993." In "Baby Bust Imprint," *Los Angeles Times,* February 9, 1989: "Nationally, the number of 18 year-olds has been declining since 1980 and will continue to drop for a few more years. . . ."

Page 111    **The value of a college degree:** " 'Reality 101': Gloom Hits Campuses as Outlook Dims," *USA Today,* May 1, 1992: "Jennifer Jordan, 21, an international affairs and economics major at George Washington University in Washington, was told she can't do much without a master's degree. At a career fair earlier this year, she heard a panelist say: 'The bachelor's of today is the equivalent of the high school diploma of the '70s.' 'Don't tell me that,' she groaned"; "Shaking The Blue Collar Blues," *Fortune,* April 22, 1991: "Eventually the market began to send a message: Why bother with college?"; "Greatly Reduced Expectations," *Rolling Stone,* March 1993: "Since at least the time of the GI Bill, the American Dream has been predicated on a trip to college. For forty years, a college degree was essential for most white-collar jobs. But current trends fly in the face of old practices. 'For college graduates entering the job market, the last couple of years have been the bleakest years we've ever seen,' says Larry Katz, a Harvard economist. Now graduating from college is a little like graduating from high school"; "Class of '91: Jubilation & Jitters," *The Washington Post,* June 11, 1991: "High school graduates with special skills, like a knowledge of plumbing or electrical work, often earn more than the estimated one-fifth of those with B.A.s who take jobs—like retail sales positions—for which no degree is required." "The American Dream and Today's Reality," *Money,* October 1992: " 'Nowadays your kid needs specific job-related training,' says Frank Levy. 'If you grew up in the 1950s or 1960s, when everything was on automatic pilot because incomes were growing fast, you might wonder why your kid can't just coast through college taking undemanding courses. But the economy isn't on automatic pilot anymore.' "

Page 114    **Fiske:** Edward B. Fiske, "Student Debt Reshaping Colleges and Careers," *The New York Times,* August 3, 1986. As Fiske explains, "Colleges are more interested in a continuing flow of new students than they are in the financial affairs of their alumni." Fiske also wrote a good history of the Guaranteed Student Loan in "Higher Education's New Economics," *The New York Times,* May 1, 1983.

Page 115  **"the program stayed small"**: "HEW's Post-Graduate Problem," *National Journal,* December 31, 1977. "Some $11.2 billion has been loaned under the program since 1965."

Page 115  **80 percent and 20 percent:** "In the academic year 1975–76, grants targeted to needy students accounted for 80 percent of all federal education aid; loans made up 17 percent (the remainder was work-study money)." Robert Kuttner, "The Patrimony Society," *The New Republic,* May 11, 1987. Kuttner quotes a College Board study on the rapidity of tuition increases: "As recently as 1980 the cost of attending four years of private university averaged about $34,000, or 118 percent of the median family income. . . . In just five years, that cost has increased to over $45,000, or 157 percent of the current median family income."

Page 115  **Graphs:** For example, "The Campus Value Line," *Time,* August 26, 1985. In the three years between 1975 and 1978, private college prices rose $1,000, from $4,000 to $5,000. In the six years after, between 1978 and 1984, costs rose $4,000, to $9,000 a year. Similarly, public college costs rose from $2,700 in 1975 to $3,100 in 1978. By 1984, they were at $4,700. Or "Costs Double in a Decade," from "Is College Worth It?," *Newsweek,* April 29, 1985.

Page 115  **Inflation:** For example, "More Help In Meeting College Costs," *Business Week,* April 11, 1977.

Page 116  **The Middle Income Student Assistance Act:** "A Break for the Rich," *Fortune,* December 18, 1978: "Oddly enough, the act specifies that henceforth there will be no income restrictions on such loans. . . . The new act [is] bad news." The results were immediately felt: "The soaring cost of the guaranteed loan program is getting out of control. Between 1978, when previous income restrictions were lifted, and now, the sum of loans has gone from $2.0 billion to $5.9 billion, and the annual cost to the Federal Government of subsidizing the program has risen from about $700 million to $3 billion." Fiske, "Higher Education's New Economics," *The New York Times,* May 1, 1983. Fiske clarifies: In 1986, "the cost of subsidizing the program headed for outer space, rising from $480 million in 1977–78 to $3.8 billion in 1984–85."

# notes

Page 117    **"By 1981"**: "College Costs: The Good News. And the Bad," *U.S. News & World Report,* April 11, 1983. "When the young matriculant returns to Old Ivy this fall, parents will likely be signing checks for an additional 10%." "Higher Education for Lower Cost," *Money,* June, 1983; "College tuitions are surging ahead at double the rate of inflation." "Is College Worth It?," *Newsweek,* April 29, 1985. Fiske reported in 1983 that "the increase is most dramatic in the private sector, where tuition at the top institutions has risen by one-third in the last three years, and where, in some cases, the annual costs may exceed $14,000." "Higher Education's New Economics," *The New York Times,* May 1, 1983.

Page 117    **"College costs diligently doubled"**: "For nine years, hikes in tuition and other fees have averaged roughly twice the cost of inflation . . . and the spiral shows no signs of stopping." "Sticker Shock at the Ivory Tower," *Time,* September 25, 1989; "College tuitions have risen at twice the rate of inflation in the past five years." Elliot Negin, *The Atlantic,* March, 1993. "Between 1980 and 1992, the tuition, room, and board for attending a private college swelled 9.2% a year—twice the rate of overall inflation and even higher than the much bemoaned medical inflation. The cost of going to a public college increased at a 7.8% annual rate." "Time to Prune the Ivy," *Business Week,* May 24, 1993.

Page 117    **" 'Tuition was one cash cow' "**: "Where Does Your Tuition Go?" *Time,* April 13, 1992.

Page 118    **"In many cases, tuitions"**: *Forbes, Time,* and *U.S. News & World Report* wrote on this paradox—Peter Brimelow, in a number of *Forbes* articles, made this his particular bête noire (e.g., "The Untouchables," *Forbes,* November 30, 1987). In "The Cost of Learning," Betsy Wagner summed up eighties increases: "The escalating expenses and tuition costs of the 1980s have led to a dangerous spiral in higher education. . . . To compensate for the shortfall, schools increased their own aid budgets by 235 percent. The cost of that institutional aid was covered, in part, by hiking tuitions. By 1990, private schools were devoting an average of 30 percent of their tuition income to scholarships, up from 20 percent a decade earlier." ("The High Cost of Learning," *U.S. News & World Report,* June 21, 1993.) *Time* from April 13, 1992: "Each time tuition went up, more incoming students required financial assistance, and many of those already paying their own way suddenly needed aid." *Newsweek* reported this as early as 1985: "One result is a particularly vicious circle: colleges raise tuition to cover their own costs, and one of the fastest-growing is often financial aid to offset the price of tuition. 'We are in for tuition increases that are higher than inflation for as far as the eye can see,' says Stanford financial-aid officer William Massey." "Is College Worth It?," *Newsweek*, April 29, 1985.

Page 118 **McPherson and Marchese:** Quoted in Fiske, "Student Debt Reshaping Colleges and Careers," *The New York Times*, August 3, 1986.

Page 118 **62 million student loans, $100 billion:** These figures appear in "Defaulting The Future," *U.S. News & World Report*, June 21, 1993. Grant-loan proportion: The College Board, 1993.

Page 119 **Default rates:** 11 percent: "Why Shouldn't College Be a Smart Investment?," *Business Week*, September 8, 1986. 22 percent: "Defaulting the Future," *U.S. News & World Report*, June 21, 1993.

Page 119 **$11.5 billion dollars in toto:** *National Journal*, December 31, 1977. $10 billion a year: *The New York Times*, "Student Debt Reshaping Colleges and Careers," August 3, 1986. $18 billion: "Nearly 8,000 banks, savings and loans, credit unions and other lenders will make an estimated $18 billion in new federally backed student loans in fiscal year 1993." "Defaulting the Future," *U.S. News & World Report*. (In comparison, the entire motion picture and video industry took in only $10 billion in 1993. "The Screening of America," *The New Yorker*, March 21, 1994.)

Page 119 **1991, $3.6 billion:** "State Loan Agencies Ranked by Student Default Rates," *The Washington Post*, August 25, 1993.

Page 119 **"only $200 million in 1980":** "The taxpayers' bill, an estimated $3.4 billion in 1992, is up from $200 million in 1980." "How You're Getting Stiffed by the Student Loan Mess," *Money*, April 1992. In the late seventies, the figure was 50 percent lower. "The government has lost almost $800 million since 1965, a sum that is increasing by at least $100 million a year." "HEW's Post-Graduate Problem," *National Journal*, December 31, 1977.

Page 119 **" 'indentured students' ":** Hanson, quoted in Fiske, "Student Debt Reshaping Colleges And Careers," *The New York Times*, August 3, 1986.

Page 120 **"We have created a new indentured class":** William Ford, quoted in "The Student Loan Mess," *Money*, April 1992.

Page 120   **"In 1993, President Clinton"**: "Clinton Plans Overhaul Of Student Loan Program," *The New York Times,* February 27, 1993. The language shows how much Clinton absorbed from the experience of the eighties. "The President has said he wants to make sure that colleges do not use the program as an excuse to increase college costs, with the knowledge that it will be easier for students to pay for college." The proposed plan is outlined in "Student Loans: A Longtime Irritation," *The New York Times,* May 2, 1993. "Now President Clinton has outlined a plan to redesign and enhance Federal student loan programs that is a simpler, cheaper and more generous approach."

Page 121   **" 'In the fifties, my parents' "**: John Brandt, "My Turn: Getting His Money's Worth," *Newsweek,* December 31, 1984.

Page 121   **"a good deal to fear"**: "Between 1985 and 1995, there will be a drop of 18% in college-age Americans . . . universities will have to scale back." "Snapshot," *Time,* September 2, 1985; "Nationally, the number of 18-year-olds has been declining since 1980 and will continue to drop for a few more years." " 'Baby Bust' Imprint; Fewer Apply at Many Private Colleges, Universities," *Los Angeles Times,* April 9, 1989; "Enrollment and demographics are major issues in higher education these days." "Colleges Combat the 'Baby Bust,' " *The Boston Globe,* August 19, 1990; "The proportion of high school graduates who go on to college soared during the past 20 years by more than a quarter to 62% in 1991." "The American Dream and Today's Reality," *Money,* October, 1992; "Area universities report their freshman classes were easier to get into than they have been in years (though they say the quality of accepted applicants stayed high)." "Shrinking Classes, Shallow Pools," *Washington Post,* July 23, 1992; "Despite the Baby Bust, universities are loosing 1.6M newly minted bachelor's, professional, and doctoral degree recipients into the job market each year, 58 percent more than during the late 1960s. Yet employment in managerial and technical fields has grown only an average of 310,000 jobs annually over the past two years, compared with an average of 1.8 million jobs each year during the 1980s. Hiring may pick up again one day, but to people coming out of degree programs now, the outlook is bleak." "Why Busters Hate Boomers," *Fortune,* October 4, 1993.

Page 121   **"price wars"**: Jane Bryant Quinn, "Cutting College Costs,"

*Newsweek,* October 1, 1984. Quinn ended, "The pricey private schools will have to offer better and better deals, or die."

Page 122   **40 percent, 53 percent:** "The number of 18-to-24-year-olds in the population is declining, from 30.4 million in 1980 to an estimated 25.8 million in 1990. But total enrollment in higher education is holding steady at about 12.4 million, and the number of institutions involved has actually increased, to an all time high of 3,340 in 1985–86. The higher education industry has been able to maintain its volume partly by reaching further down into its traditional market. In recent years some 62% of graduating high school seniors have gone on to higher education, compared with 52.5% 20 years earlier and less than 40% before 1950." "The Untouchables," *Forbes,* November 30, 1987. Victor Fuchs had warned of the drop in students: "Between 1980 and 1990 the population at ages 15–24 will decline by approximately 15%. The decrease in the number of college-age youth will put higher education in financial jeopardy." Victor Fuchs, *How We Live,* p. 227. According to "The Value of College," *Newsweek,* August 31, 1992, the number of college graduates almost doubled between 1969 and 1990: from 12.6 percent of all U.S. workers to 23.2 percent in 1990. The percentage of high school graduates went up by one point, from 38.4 percent to 39.4 percent.

Page 122   " **'paying customers'** ": "Class of '91: Jubilation and Jitters," *The Washington Post,* June 11, 1991. "Even the top colleges have had to resort to more aggressive recruiting and to draw deeper into their waiting lists to offset the dual affects of the baby bust and the financial crunch."

Page 122   **"A 1992 congressional study":** "Student Loan Mess," *Money,* April 1992.

Page 123   ***gumption":*** "When Financial Aid Is Not Enough," *Money,* September, 1986. "The old-fashioned work ethic is now the craze on campus. While those who pay their own way completely are rare, more than half of all full-time students are employed, with 28% working as many as 21 to 35 hours a week. Usually a student's financial aid package . . . covers only 28% of all costs. Students generally pay 33% of the tab, frequently by means of jobs they get on their own initiative."

Page 123   " **'immaturity,' 'indecision'** ": "Today's Graduates May Be

Too Young at Heart," *People,* May 19, 1986 (compare with *Money,* above.) "Q. You say kids are taking longer to complete college. Is that a sign of putting off adult responsibility? A. At most urban universities, the average student takes five and a half years to get a diploma. The biggest reason is that these kids are less committed and less directed than their parents were." "The Society," *The Public Perspective,* The Roper Center for Public Opinion Research, September/October 1990. Because "recent data from the Department of Education indicates that the majority of college students no longer graduate in four years," the "new generation appears less anxious to enter the job market." See also "The Boomerang Age," American *Demographics,* May 1987.

Page 123 **"their 'futures were mortgaged' "**: Quoted in "Graduating College Seniors Face School of Hard Knocks," *The Washington Post,* May 5, 1991.

## v. musical chairs

Page 131 **"Some socioeconomic event"**: Fuchs, *How We Live,* p. 92.

Page 133 **" 'Of all the icy winds' "**: Gustave Flaubert, *Madame Bovary,* trans. Francis Steegmuller, (New York: Random House, 1957; first published, 1857).

Page 133 **"In the 1930s"**: *Historical Statistics of the United States, Colonial Times to 1970.* (Washington, D.C.: U.S. Government Printing Office, 1975) (p. 64). The single lowest marriage rate in the century was recorded in 1932—7.9 marriages per 1,000. The single biggest two-year drop (discounting the inflated war marriages of 1946, when the rate ballooned to 16.4 per 1,000) was from 1929 to 1931, the years just after the Depression.

Page 133 **22.6, 20.3**: "Young Adults Return to Nest," *USA Today,* February 12, 1993. Also, "Sex in the '90s," *The Washington Post,* January 8, 1989: " 'Today, young people are postponing marriage for so long,' writes Martha Farnsworth Riche, 'that an unprecedented number will never marry at all.' "

Page 133 **"already the highest in the century"**: "The Unromantic Generation," *The New York Times Magazine,* April 5, 1987.

Page 133 **Mid-twenties**: In the 1970 census, 36 percent of women and 55 percent of men in the 20 to 24 age group had never married; by

1983, those proportions had risen to 56 percent and 73 percent. By the 1988 census, those proportions had risen to 61 percent and 77 percent—54.5 percent higher than 1970. By the 1990 census, the numbers were 63 percent and 79 percent—a 60 percent increase over 1970. Similarly, the timing of first births shifted between 1970 and 1987. In "Postponed, but Not Forgotten," *American Demographics,* July 1991, a study by the Population Reference Board of University of Wisconsin showed that the majority of first births in 1970 took place at age 24. The majority of first births in 1987 took place at age 28.

Page 134   **"By 1987, there were half as many"**: "Mysterious Young Adults," *American Demographics,* February 1987. In an article called "Disappearing Act," the magazine asked: "Where have all the couples gone? The Baby Bust [generation], following on the heels of the baby boom, is affecting household living arrangements. The 1990 census should show that the number of married couples headed by people under age 25 has declined fully 46% in five years." "Disappearing Act," *American Demographics,* January 1989.

Page 134   **"The twenty-five to thirty bracket"**: "What 25-Year-Olds Want," *Fortune,* August 27, 1990. See also "Marrying Age Higher Than Ever Before," *USA Today,* June 7, 1991. "The median age for first marriage is 26.1 for men, 23.9 for women, the highest since the Census Bureau started keeping track in 1890."

Page 134   **Spring 1993 census**: In a February 12, 1993, article discussing these (again high-water-mark) numbers, the *Atlanta Journal-Constitution* explained, "Many people hold the 1950s image of a married couple in their mid-20s as the norm for American society. In the mid-1950s, when America's economy was in the midst of an unprecedented era of growth, the typical man got married at 22.6 years of age. 'People's idea of what's normal is what they saw when they grew up,' said Martha Farnsworth Riche, director of policy studies at the Population Reference Bureau in Washington. But as the statistics on the age of marriage show, that period actually was an unusual blip in history. The economy was so strong then that it would be virtually impossible for the baby busters to do better than their parents. 'Their parents' generation made a killing,' Ms. Riche said. 'We're now back on a long-term track.' " As Stefanie Harris, a twenty-three-year-old graduate, told the paper, "It takes longer to get established, so you don't even think about being committed to a relationship. You try to keep yourself open to any opportunity that becomes available."

Page 134 **Minnesota Survey:** "Tough Economic Times Produce a New Generation of Realists," *Minneapolis Star Tribune,* December 28, 1991.

Page 134 **"The newspaper and magazine people":** "No Money, No Marry," *American Demographics,* December 1991; "Drop in Births Reported, and Recession Is Blamed," *The New York Times,* November 3, 1991: "Marriages also fell 2 percent in the first seven months of 1991, the department said . . . economists and demographers generally agreed that the decline in births and marriages was significant and was caused by the 16-month recession[.] Said Carl Haub, the director of demographic analysis for the Population Research Bureau, a private company in Washington, "The faith of young couples in the job outlook and the economy has been shaken." On October 19, 1992, *U.S. News & World Report* ran an article called "Love and Money": "Said Douglas Besharov, resident scholar at the American Enterprise Institute, 'The bottom line is that family composition and family dynamics are uniquely intertwined with macroeconomic conditions.' . . . Barbara Foley Wilson, a National Center for Health Statistics demographer who specializes in marriage, says that the relationship between the economy and marriage has been recognized for decades." The article described young adults as "Waiting to Wed." One twenty-seven-year-old explained he and his girlfriend are "biding their time . . . as he continues looking for full-time work. 'We're ready to move on,' said [the young man], 'but I can't without the job security.' " A young woman explained that she was stretching her engagement after "losing her public-relations job in June, 1991 and then failing in her attempt to start her own business." Said the woman, "I had been blown out of the water. It made me feel like I wanted time." As *U.S. News* put it, "Young couples who are still planning their families seem very aware of the trials of raising children in an uncertain economy."

Page 135 **Julia Carlisle:** "Young, Privileged and Unemployed," *The New York Times,* April 4, 1991.

Page 136 **" 'a remarkable generational distress' ":** Howe and Strauss, *Generations,* p. 320. Quoted in each version of Howe and Strauss (*13th Gen, The Atlantic's* "New Generation Gap"); originally in "Our Sheltered Political Class," Robert Kuttner, *The Washington Post,* August 31, 1990.

Page 136   **Sexual revolution ended:** As of the early eighties: "Is Promiscuity Passé?" *Harper's Bazaar,* June 1982; "The Case for Staying Faithful," *Mademoiselle,* June 1982; "From Cheating to Commitment: Why I Now Believe in Fidelity," *Glamour,* July 1982; "The New Scarlet Letter," *Time,* August 2, 1982; "The Herpes Threat: Why Casual Sex Isn't Casual Anymore," *McCall's,* September 1982; "Love's Labors Lost," *Esquire,* November 1982; "Is Sex Dead? *New York,* December 6, 1982; "The End of Sex," *Esquire,* December 1982; and "The Revolution Is Over," *Time,* April 9, 1984. After AIDS appeared in the heterosexual community (its appearance within the homosexual community was apparently no great concern), the cycle began again: "Is Sex Dead? The AIDS Hot Line," *Harper's Bazaar,* March 1986; "Kiss Me Deadly," *Mademoiselle,* May 1986; "Fear of Sex," *Newsweek,* November 24, 1986; etc.

Page 139   " **'There's a great sense of chaos' ":** "For Lovers, Number One Activity These Days Is Worrying," *The New York Times,* February 12, 1992. See also Simon Montefiore, "Love, Lies, and Fear in the Plague Years: Sex in the 1990s," *Psychology Today,* September 1992. Montefiore explains, "Despite what the media hipsters say, casual sex is alive and well among the twentysomething set. . . . In the world of sex, the editors and feature writers have created a completely mythical, modern world of sexless twentysomethings." He continues, "Are we afraid of catching AIDS? Of course we are. No gathering of twentysomethings is completely without an AIDS discussion, and without members telling each other that, while they know the risks, they themselves are not in danger." Says Montefiore, "If orgasm, as the French call it, is the 'petit mort,' AIDS is the Big Death. Death and Sex are indelibly stamped together like a tattoo on the skin of my generation." His prose turns into a James Bond novel at the end. "The underground of sexual adventure has become a dangerous sex casino where love, lies, and fear are a perpetual threesome in the bedrooms of America."

Page 142   **55 percent of all consumer spending:** "Business's best customers are still 'traditional' families. Married-couple families account for 55% of all U.S. households. Married couple families also account for 70% of total consumer spending. The biggest spenders [are] married couples with children under 18." "Receipts from a Marriage," *American Demographics,* February 1993.

Page 142   **20 percent of GDP:** "Q. Just how important are these 'household starts' to the economy as a whole? A. They represent the largest component of service consumption. Direct and indirect housing expenditures account for roughly one-fifth of total GNP." "The Death of Growth? Demographer Sees a Radical Change in Vital Trends," *Barron's,* January 7, 1991.

Page 142  **Hokenson:** "For Home builders, the Wolf Is at the Door . . . but an Even Bleaker Future May Be Looming," *Business Week,* July 3, 1989; "Wall Street: Consumer Driven? Not This Economy," *The New York Times,* December 6, 1990; "Analyst Looks to Family Trends to Guide Wall Street," *USA Today,* April 22, 1991; "What Will Lead to Recovery?," *Fortune,* May 11, 1991; "Young Adults to the Rescue," *Philadelphia Inquirer,* September 25, 1992.

Page 142  **Household formation:** "The Death of Growth?," *Barron's:* "In the current recession [a] person over 25 who might have left home and started his own household in good times is less likely to do so when their salary is lower or employment is less certain. Plus, you have people who return home—what's called the baby-boomerangers. And that is likely to increase during recession. The first glimpse that we saw of that was during the 81–82 recession. . . . This time around, growth has already slowed to a crawl even before the recession began. Household formations grew 0.56% last year—that's about the level they dropped to during the Great Depression."

Page 143  **" 'Every generation' ":** "What Happened to the American Dream?" *Business Week,* August 19, 1991. "It is no doubt premature to condemn the Baby-Bust generation to permanently lower living standards. But it seems increasingly likely that America's young people are going to mature in a less affluent world. And that spells trouble for all Americans, young and old alike."

Page 144  **" 'I have no panacea' ":** Bryan J. Burket, "Brother, Can You Spare a Job? What They Didn't Teach About Surviving a Recession," *The Washington Post,* May 12, 1991.

Page 145  **Late children:** "Older Parents: Good for Kids?," *Time,* October 10, 1988: "There is plenty of evidence that late children often have problems that other kids do not face. [In] a new study of 22 adult children of older parents, sociologist Monica Morris of California State University, Los Angeles, found that only two of her subjects would wholeheartedly choose to have their children later in life. The others unleashed a litany of lateborn woes. They said older parents, usually fearful of physical injury and health problems themselves, were often reluctant to participate in games and sports. . . . 'No doubt, having children earlier is better and later is worse,' says Yale psychologist Edward Zigler. 'Children are always a blessing and a trial.' " The article turns grimly funny, "It is no secret that children may be embarrassed by their parents' gray hair, their outmoded clothes and opinions that may seem as antediluvian as dinosaurs. And parental physical incompetence can be mortifying. For Tom McDonough, 49, the memory of playing baseball with his 58-year-old father is especially painful. 'I said, "Dad, run, run." He dropped the bat and looked at me and said, "I can't." ' " According to *Time,* the number of over-35 first-time births had "quadrupled in the past decade, and is expected to increase further in the next few years."

Page 146  " '**music of being single**' ": Lorrie Moore, *Anagrams: A Novel* (New York: Knopf, 1986).

## vi. in situ parentis

Page 153  **"up by 20 percent"**: "Have Degree, Will Travel," *Time,* June 6, 1983. Similarly, students began moving home. One graduate told *The New York Times* in 1982, " 'I've got a 3.7 grade point, and I still can't find a job.' She said that if she could not find a job, she would move back to her parents' home in the Bronx and consider going to law school next year." "New Graduates Said to Find Fewer Offers of Employment," *The New York Times,* May 24, 1982.

Page 153  **Law school applications:** "Some See Graduate School as Haven in Slow Economy," *Los Angeles Times,* July 24, 1991. As the *Times* continued, "America's new college graduates have found a way to get around the current U.S. job market slump: They are flocking to enroll in graduate schools to mark time until the economy improves. 'Graduate schools are nice places to hide out,' notes Victor Lindquist, editor of the Lindquist-Endicott Report, an annual survey of employment trends for college graduates. Many graduate students concede they would not be in school now if the economy were robust." See also "With Jobs Scarce, Many Turn to Graduate School," *The New York Times,* July 3, 1991.

Page 153 **"half of all graduating"**: "The Terrible Twenties," *Chicago Tribune,* February 13, 1992. "At many leading graduate and law schools an estimated one-half to two-thirds of the Class of 1992 have no jobs in store for them after graduation." In fact, at the nation's largest law firms, there had been almost no new net hiring since 1990. "Job Outlook Bleak at Big Law Firms," *The New York Times,* May 7, 1993: "[This] continues a trend that many business experts thought had hit bottom in 1991. . . . Although the recession is over and legal business appears to be recovering from its effects, the firms are continuing to lay off lawyers and freeze hiring because there is no longer enough work to support the number of lawyers they employed in the booming 1980's. . . . Growth at the nation's 500 largest firms was flatter than it had been since the 1950's and early 1960's. . . . 'We were stunned after we did the math,' [said the managing editor for the law magazine *Counsel*]. 'For the modern era of law firms, this kind of flat growth is unprecedented.' "

Page 153 **"The number of college students intending"**: "Freshman Aspirations Hit Records," *The American Freshman: National Norms for Fall 1993,* from the Higher Education Research Institute. p. 2. This is the highest proportion ever recorded by the institute. In the early seventies that number had been "below 50." The number held steady through that decade. Also, "New College Freshmen Show Shifts In Attitudes," *The New York Times,* January 9, 1989: By 1980, only 48.3% of freshman had intended to pursue advanced degrees. By 1989, that number had bounced to 58.7, what the *Times* then called a "record proportion."

Page 153 **Graduate Record Exam:** "Better by Degrees: College Grads Seeking Career Edge by Staying in School," *Newsday,* May 9, 1993.

Page 153 **Medical schools:** "Medical Schools Gaining an Unexpected Popularity," *The New York Times,* May 18, 1993: "Beginning with applications for the 1990–91 year, the increase has been steady, reflecting a stunning reversal of the decline in popularity of medicine as a profession among young Americans. As recently as 1988, applications to medical schools had plunged to the lowest level since 1970. . . . Medical and educational leaders interviewed said they were puzzled by the rapid turnaround in the popularity of a medicine as a career. But the applicants themselves, as well as officials of medical schools and colleges, offered a number of explanations for the turnaround in interviews. . . . Medicine, they say, offers both a degree of economic security and, in viewing health as a way to help people, a chance to do good for the community. . . . Applicants are also realistic. In a generally inhospitable job market, they see medicine as a surer way of earning an income. . . . Medicine, said the director of admissions at Harvard Medical School, is seen as recession-proof."

Page 153 **"best year ever"**: "Big Recovery Cited in Medical School Applications," *The Boston Globe,* May 19, 1993. "Applications for the fall of 1994 will break the record if the increase in the number of people taking the Medical College Admissions Test this year is an indication, up by 3,000 over 1992, according to Dr. Edward J. Stemmler, AAMC executive vice president." The record, of 64,000, was set in 1974.

Page 153 **"In Prague"**: "Y(oung) A(mericans in) P(rague)," *The New York Times Magazine,* December 12, 1993. See also ". . . All They Are Saying Is Give Prague a Chance," *Smithsonian,* June 1993.

Page 153 **Japan:** "Job Search Takes Many to Japan; Country Courts Americans to Teach Western Ways," *Seattle Times,* October 11, 1992. "For a growing number of young Americans, some frustrated by the lack of jobs here . . . Japan has become a favored destination. . . . As Japan adjusts to its new role on the world stage, Americans have become the hired tutors in the country's crash course on Western ways. There are now about 40,000 non-military Americans working in Japan, according to an official with the American Embassy in Tokyo. 'It has really mushroomed over the past 10 years,' the embassy spokesman said. 'The number of Americans working here 20 years ago is negligible compared to the number of people here now.' "

Page 153 **Moscow:** "The Yupskies Are Coming," *New York,* August 2, 1993. "Demoralized by the lack of opportunity he found in America, [twenty-three-year-old] Gregg Gershuny traded New York for Moscow. He relocated in February, planning to stay a few months—just long enough to jump-start his career. He's not coming home. 'There's too much going on here,' Gershuny says. Within two months, he found work as a development manager for a prominent international vodka company. 'I'm 23, I've been here five months, and I went from having to beg for work to coming here and making more than a college grad.' He even has a car. 'One year here,' he insists, 'is worth five in the States.' "

Page 153 **" 'Everyone's overqualified' "**: "Young Americans Flock to Prague: Job Opportunities, Fun, Plentiful in 'Left Bank of the 1990s,' "

*The Houston Chronicle,* September 13, 1992. "Despite rising prices, Prague is still the kind of place where, in the words of one young American, 'if you have $1,000 in savings saved up, that can last eight months.' 'A friend of mine said if I came here with $100 I would have a job before I spent it,' said Ross Larsen as he puffed on a cigarette in the stairway of a former Communist Party building in the center of Prague. 'He said it was a really beautiful place.' [P]roving his friend right, he soon landed a job at the English-language Prague Post where he has interviewed prime ministers and Supreme Court justices and risen to become assistant news editor. He makes just $400 a month but pays only $75 a month for rent and just became engaged to his Czech girlfriend."

Page 154   " **'Someone described it to me' ":** "In Prague, Americans Find Land of Opportunity," *The Boston Globe,* September 7, 1992. See also "For Some Young Americans, Prague Is the Place to Wait Out Recession. It's a 'Left Bank of the 90s,' a Land of Opportunity," *Los Angeles Times,* January 13, 1992. " 'The place has tremendous appeal,' says Roberta Wilson, [twenty-four]. 'I was home last fall, and you could feel the country sagging—no jobs, worry about the recession, no sense of direction.' "

Page 154   **"Today's young adults—if they spread their wings at all— are flying back home in flocks":** "The Younger Generation That Never Grew Up," *Los Angeles Times,* April 17, 1986.

Page 154   **Boomeranging:** "The Boomerang Age," *American Demographics,* May, 1990. *American Demographics* had covered the subject as well in "Mysterious Young Adults," February 1987; "Up the Down Staircase," April 1989. The phenomenon of young people moving back was surprising and repellent. *Newsweek* found some space for it in their "Year of the Yuppie" cover story on December 31, 1984. See also "Slack Economy Forces Some Young Couples to Move In with Parents," *The Christian Science Monitor* March 23, 1983. The first mention of "boomeranging" in the eighties can be seen in a *Time* magazine article. "The Prodigals Return," *Time,* October 13, 1980.

Page 155   **"Three quarters of all young men":** Reported in "The Boomerang Age," *American Demographics:* "More young adults are living with their parents than at any time since the Depression. . . . It doesn't make sense to call someone an adult if they don't live independently. . . . Only 25 percent of young men live independently, and only 38 percent of young women do." This was repeated in "Proceeding with Caution," *Time,* as: "Fully 75% of young males 18 to 24 years old are still living at home, the largest proportion since the Great Depression."

Page 156  **1960 census:** "What You Really Owe Your Kids," *Money,* June 1988. Forty-three percent of 18–24-year-olds lived at home in 1960, nine percent of 25–34-year-olds. Twenty years later, in 1980, the first number was relatively unchanged. Forty-eight percent were at home. ("Behind The Bulge," *Los Angeles Times,* June 17, 1990.) Within 3 decades, the last number had doubled ("Nest Dwellers," *San Francisco Chronicle,* February 15, 1993). "[According to the census], in the 25-to-34 age bracket the proportion of stay-at-homes doubled in a 32-year span." As *The Boston Globe* put it, "Fifteen years ago, it wouldn't have happened. Ten years ago, it would have been called dweebish, an admission of failure." "You Can Go Home Again," *The Boston Globe,* July 24, 1992.

Page 156  *American Demographics:* "Boomerang Age." In "Mysterious Young Adults," February 1987, the magazine had said, "Living with Mom and Dad does not fit the image people have of young adults, nor does it match with how young adults think they will live. Among high school seniors in 1980, for example, 75% of the men and 65% of the women expected to live independently before marriage. But a minority of young adults live alone or with nonrelatives." Katherine Boo, writing in *The Washington Monthly,* put it more bluntly: "Many of us would feel more comfortable at a Washington party asserting we were in a methadone program with a battering spouse than confessing we still lived with mom." Yet, "It's a pandemic so ominous that 'doubling up'—relatives sharing space—has even earned a label from social statisticians: 'Borderline Homeless.' America's adult children are coming home in droves for the first time since World War II, and that seems to us a serious violation of the natural way of life." Katherine Boo, "Grow Up, Twenty-Somethings, You Can Go Home Again," *The Washington Monthly,* April, 1992.

Page 156  **"A sociologist":** Allan Schnaiberg, quoted in "Guess Who's Staying for Dinner?" *People,* August 12, 1991. "Q: Are men or women more likely to be boomerang kids? A: Men, in part because the median age at which they get married these days is 26 or 27, several years later than most young women." Jane Bryant Quinn also reached this conclusion in "What's for Dinner, Mom?" *Newsweek,* April 5, 1993. "The reason more men are at home than women may not (or not *only*) be that they won't learn to sew on buttons but that men are more likely to be single." *The New York Times* suggested other explanations. "Among 25-to-34-year-olds, 32 percent of single men and 20 percent of single women were living with their parents last year. There are few hard explanations for the wide disparity between men and women. Demographers speculate that men find living at home more attractive than women do because they are less skilled at setting up their own households, enjoy the pampering of their mothers and suffer virtually no loss of independence. Divorce rates are rising among parents, and mothers who would otherwise be living alone may value the protection and companionship of an adult son." "More Young Single Men Hang Onto Apron Strings," *The New York Times,* June 16, 1991.

Page 157   **1993 census:** U.S. Census, 1993. Ages twenty-two to twenty-four; 58 percent; Ages twenty-five to twenty-nine: 30 percent; Ages thirty to thirty-four: 23 percent. Quoted in "A Generation on Hold: More Young Adults Are Living at Home Because They Can't Afford to Go On Their Own, the Census Bureau Says," *Atlanta Journal-Constitution,* February 12, 1993. "America's baby busters continue to set records for delaying marriage and parenthood. But if you ask these trendsetters why they're putting family values on hold, they won't offer an explanation of individual freedom and experimentation—they left that to their baby-boomer parents. This generation of Americans has a hard-luck story to tell. Gaining an economic foothold has become so difficult today that the majority of young, single adults—aged 20–24—still lived with their parents in 1992." A 1992 *American Demographics* article ("Hanging Out with American Youth") explained, "Increases in the cost of living, combined with a decline in real wages during the 1980s, have created a new market niche. Nearly 20 million live-at-home young adults are now 'pre-adults,' a new life stage in an increasingly uncertain era." This despite polls like the following: "After children turn 18, should they live away from their parents? Yes: 69%. No: 29%. Not Sure: 2%." "USA Snapshot," *USA Today,* June 17, 1993.

Page 158   **" 'If you graduated' ":** Allan Schnaiberg, as quoted in "Guess Who's Staying for Dinner?" *People,* August 12, 1991. Schnaiberg published one of the first studies on boomerang kids, whom he called

ILYAs—Incompletely Launched Young Adults. In 1987, he explained to *Advertising Age,* " 'The middle and upper-middle class defines a successful young adult as one who spreads his wings: graduates college, finds an apartment, gets a job and starts developing a serious relationship. But today that's just too much to ask, given the economy. . . . We're seeing the end of an era, where the kids could move off and there was enough to go around,' the professor said in a recent interview. . . . Under such tension, something's got to give. In this case, Mr. Schnaiberg and his colleagues believe it will be great expectations. Instead of expecting a child to find a mate, career and house, parents will expect maybe two out of three—maybe less. And so will the children. Success will be redefined. Instead of emphasizing the rewards of a challenging career, parents will begin pointing out the reduced stress of so-called undemanding jobs. Parents also may start to praise the value of friendship and closeness over material success." "Young Adults Crowd 'Empty Nest,' " *Advertising Age,* March 9, 1987.

Page 158   **The *Times*'s strong stance:** "Parents Who Still Control," *The New York Times,* September 5, 1985: "It's not that parents think of their adult children as stupid and incompetent." Also, "Relationships: Children In Debt to Parents," *The New York Times,* July 6, 1987: "There is also the notion of appropriateness. 'Children must understand that it is inappropriate to ask for money to finance something they should have budgeted for,' Gershenfeld said. 'Nor should they expect parents to sacrifice their own plans to finance the child's wants.' Parents, she continued, 'must recognize that saying "no" will not make them less of a parent, and that saying "yes" won't buy their children's love or respect.' "

Page 158   " **'your child is a disappointment'** ": "Parent and Child," *The New York Times,* May 27, 1993. The article goes on, as Schnaiberg had predicted in 1987: "Parents' aspirations for their children also change as they take into account the differences between the social and economic pressures they faced as young adults and those their children face. Today's young adults will probably marry and have children later than their parents did. They're less able to buy a house without help and more likely to come back to their parents' home to live. Still, there are parents who stick to their own agendas for their children's lives. . . . 'Parents have to take responsibility for their own feelings of disappointment,' Dr. Sandra J. Eller said. 'There's often grieving that comes along with letting go of some of those dreams.' "

## vii. conclusion

Page 172 **"In the optimistic scenario"**: "The Entertainment Economy," *Business Week,* March 14, 1994.

Page 172–73 **Smallweed, Carstone:** Charles Dickens, *Bleak House* (1853; London: Penguin, 1971). Smallweed: pp. 342, 344. Carstone: pp. 583, 751–52. On Carstone: "I had a tormenting idea that he was postponing his best truth and earnestness until the suit should be off his mind."

# Permissions Acknowledgments

Grateful acknowledgment is made to the following for permission to reprint previously published material:

*Advertising Age:* Excerpt from "Young Adults Crowd 'Empty Nest' " by Lenore Skenazy from the March 9, 1987, issue of *Advertising Age.* Copyright, Crain Communications Inc., 1987. Reprinted by permission of *Advertising Age.*

*The Atlanta Journal* and *The Atlanta Constitution:* Excerpts and paraphrasing from "A Generation on Hold: More Young Adults Are Living at Home Because They Can't Afford to Go on Their Own, the Census Bureau Says" by Carrie Teegardin (February 12, 1993, page F-1) and "Growing Up Southern: The Kids Take Over—The child of the '90s Is a New Kind of Hazel, Cleaning the House, Looking After Siblings and Doing the Grocery Shopping While Mom and Dad Are at Work" by Carrie Teegardin (June 7, 1993, page E-1). Reprinted with the permission from *The Atlanta Journal* and *The Atlanta Constitution.*

*Barron's:* Excerpt from "The Death of Growth" from the January 7, 1991, issue of *Barron's.* Copyright © 1991 by Dow Jones & Company, Inc. All rights reserved worldwide. Reprinted by permission of *Barron's.*

*The Christian Science Monitor:* Excerpts from "Has Road to Adulthood Suddenly Gotten Longer?" by Lisa Lane from the March 13, 1986, issue of *The Christian Science Monitor.* Reprinted by permission.

*Forbes:* Excerpt from "The Untouchables" by Peter Brimelow from the November 30, 1987, issue of *Forbes.* Copyright © 1987 by Forbes, Inc. Reprinted by permission of *Forbes* magazine.

*Fortune:* Excerpts from "The Baby Bust Hits the Job Market" from the May 27, 1985, issue of *Fortune.* Copyright © 1985 by Time, Inc. All rights reserved. Reprinted by permission.

GOVERNOR RICHARD LAMM: Excerpt from "Borrowing from Our Children" by Richard Lamm from the May 29, 1985, issue of *The Christian Science Monitor.* Reprinted by permission.

*The New Yorker:* Excerpt from "The Sorcerer's Apprentices" by Sidney Blumenthal from the July 19, 1993, issue of *The New Yorker.* First published in *The New Yorker.* Copyright © 1993 by Sidney Blumenthal. Reprinted by permission.

*The New York Times:* Excerpts from "Just How Serious Are Deficit Dangers" by Edward Cowan (October 23, 1983), "Student Debt Reshaping Colleges and Careers" by Edward B. Fiske (August 3, 1986), "The Unromantic Generation: Alone Together" by Bruce Weber (April 5, 1987), "The Price They Pay: Older Children and Divorce" by Barbara S. Cain (February 18, 1990), and "Parent and Child" by Lawrence Kutner (October 3, 1991). Copyright © 1983, 1986, 1987, 1990, 1991 by The New York Times Company. Reprinted by permission.

## About the Authors

DAVID LIPSKY graduated from Brown University. His work has appeared in *The New Yorker, The New York Times, Harper's Magazine, Rolling Stone, Details, The Best American Short Stories,* and many others. His collection of fiction, *Three Thousand Dollars,* was published in 1989; his first novel will be published by Doubleday. He teaches at The Johns Hopkins University and lives in New York City.

ALEXANDER ABRAMS graduated from Brown University. He has worked for NBC News and as a member of the advance staff for President Clinton's election campaign. He has spoken on young people in a variety of forums, including ABC, Fox Television, and CNN. He is an attorney and lives in New York City.